JENKINS GARRETT LIBRARY
TARRANT COUNTY COLLEGE
5301 CAMPUS DRIVE
FORT WORTH TEXAS 76119

THE NEW DEAL

FIFTY YEARS AFTER

A Historical Assessment

Edited by Wilbur J. Cohen

LYNDON BAINES JOHNSON LIBRARY

LYNDON B. JOHNSON SCHOOL OF PUBLIC AFFAIRS

Library of Congress Catalog Card No.:84-82347
ISBN: 0-89940-415-4
© 1984 by the Board of Regents
The University of Texas
Printed in the U.S.A.
Funding provided by the Lyndon Baines Johnson Foundation
Design by Barbara Jezek

Photo credits: cover, Wide World Photos; p. 50,
UPI/Bettmann Archives; p. 51 (top) Franklin D. Roosevelt
Library Collection; p. 51 (bottom) Wide World Photos.
Photos of conference participants provided by the Lyndon
Baines Johnson Library/Museum and the UT News and
Information Service.

To the many participants in the New Deal,
who provided inspiring leadership in
a crucial historic period in the United States.

CONTENTS

PREFACE	vii
PARTICIPANTS	ix
INTRODUCTION	xxi
WELCOME	3
Harry Middleton	3
Mrs. Lyndon B. Johnson	4
I. HOW IT ALL BEGAN	7
Looking Back: Roosevelt's New Deal in the Making	11
John Kenneth Galbraith	
Panel Presentations	19
Wilbur J. Cohen, Chair	19
Virginia Durr	20
Page Keeton	23
Leon Keyserling	24
James Rowe	27
Esther Van Wagoner Tufty	28
William S. White	30
John Houseman	32
Questions from the Audience	34
Rapporteur's Summary	38
Ernest L. Cuneo	
II. FRANKLIN ROOSEVELT: THE MAN BEHIND THE NEW DEAL	41
Reminiscences of Franklin Roosevelt	44
James Roosevelt	
Introduction of Special Guest	57
Elspeth Rostow	
Richard Tallboys	57
III. THE POST-NEW DEAL ERA	61
The Shadow of FDR: Presidents from Truman to Reagan	63
William E. Leuchtenburg	

Panel Presentations	75
Elspeth Rostow	75
Katie Louchheim, Chair	75
Frank Freidel	76
Charles McLaughlin	78
Clarence Mitchell	81
George Nash	86
Questions from the Audience	90
Rapporteur's Summary	93
Douglass Cater	
IV. THE NEW DEAL'S LEGACY FOR THE FUTURE	97
A President's View of the New Deal	99
Gerald R. Ford	
The Education Dimension of the New Deal Legacy	106
John Brademas	
Panel Presentations	119
Douglass Cater, Chair	119
Vernon Jordan	119
Jack Kemp	120
Mary Keyserling	122
Claude Pepper	124
William Rusher	125
Esther Peterson	127
Jennings Randolph	128
Panel Discussion	130
V. CONCLUSION	143
Conference Summary	144
Elspeth Rostow	
Preserving the Legacies of the New Deal	147
Charles S. Robb	

PREFACE

This volume is the product of a symposium held in March 1983 under the auspices of the Lyndon Baines Johnson Library/Museum, the Franklin Delano Roosevelt Library, Virginia Commonwealth University, and The University of Texas at Austin. The event, which coincided with the fiftieth anniversary of Franklin D. Roosevelt's first inauguration on March 4, 1933, owed its success to the efforts of many people from all these institutions. Special thanks are due to Professor Melvin Urofsky of Virginia Commonwealth University, Elspeth Rostow, then Dean of the LBJ School of Public Affairs, and Harry J. Middleton, Director of the LBJ Library/Museum, whose support made the symposium a reality.

In Austin, the event was coordinated by a planning committee chaired by Elspeth Rostow. Members included Robert L. Hardesty, President of Southwest State University; Barbara Jordan, Lyndon B. Johnson Centennial Chair in National Policy, LBJ School of Public Affairs; Lorrin Kennamer, Dean of the College of Education, UT Austin; Lowell H. Lebermann, Jr., President of Centex Beverage, Inc. (Austin); Robert D. Mettlan, Vice President for Administration, UT Austin; Harry J. Middleton, Director of the LBJ Library/Museum; Stephen A. Monti, Assistant to the President of UT Austin; Shirley Bird Perry, then Vice President and Coordinator of Centennial Program Activities at UT Austin; Melvin P. Sikes, Professor of Educational Psychology at UT Austin; Jerre S. Williams, Judge, U.S. Court of Appeals for the 5th Circuit; and J. Sam Winters, Attorney with Clark, Thomas, Winters, and Shapiro. Consultants to the committee included, in addition to myself, Elizabeth Carpenter of the LBJ Library/Museum, and Emmette S. Redford, Ashbel Smith Professor at the LBJ School.

Because the gathering of so many New Deal participants and observers was in itself a historically significant event, the symposium coordinators made provisions to preserve it through publication. As editor, I assumed responsibility for seeing that the transcripts were "polished" into a readable form. This process necessarily included some condensation and refinement, but the aim was always to enhance rather than to alter the spirit and substance of the discussions. In fulfilling this editorial responsibility I worked closely with Marilyn Duncan of the LBJ School Office of Publications. That office also handled the production phases of the project.

The result of these efforts is, we hope, a book that will stimulate and enlighten its readers while conveying a sense of the enduring significance of the New Deal and its legacies.

Wilbur J. Cohen

PARTICIPANTS

JOHN BRADEMAS, currently President of New York University, served in the U.S. Congress for twenty-two years as Representative (Democrat) from Indiana's Third District. From 1976 to 1980, he served as House Majority Whip, third-ranking member of the Majority Leadership. During his twenty-two years of service on the House Education and Labor Committee, Dr. Brademas helped write most of the major legislation concerning elementary and secondary education, higher education, vocational education, services for the elderly and handicapped, and federal support for libraries, museums, and the arts and humanities.

In addition to his present position as university president, he serves as Chairman of the Board of Directors of the Federal Reserve Bank of New York and as a member of the boards of directors of several organizations, including the New York Stock Exchange and the Rockefeller Foundation.

DOUGLASS CATER is President of Washington College in Chestertown, Maryland. As Special Assistant to President Lyndon B. Johnson, he collaborated on many educational initiatives that became law, including the Higher Education Act, the Elementary and Secondary Education Act, and the International Education Act. He is a charter member of the Paideia Project on education and a Founding Fellow and Trustee of the Aspen Institute for Humanistic Studies.

Mr. Cater was Washington Editor and later National Affairs Editor for *Reporter Magazine* from 1950 to 1964. Until 1981 he was Vice-Chairman of England's oldest weekly newspaper, the *Observer*. He is author or coauthor of seven books on a variety of topics related to ethics and power in government.

ERNEST L. CUNEO, a prominent lawyer and journalist, began his career as law secretary to Fiorello LaGuardia in the 1930s. Now a military analyst and columnist for the North American Newspaper Alliance, Mr. Cuneo served as that organization's president and board chairman from 1960 to 1965. He is also a past director of Freedom House and the Woodrow Wilson Institute for International Scholars. Among his publications are *Life with Fiorello* and two studies of the dynamics of history.

VIRGINIA FOSTER DURR, a native of Alabama, became associated with the New Deal when her husband Clifford went to Washington, D.C., to work for the Reconstruction Finance Corporation in the reopening of the nation's banks. The Durrs' home in Alexandria, Virginia, became a center for Southern liberals drawn to Washington by FDR, and Mrs. Durr became active in a variety of liberal organizations. She was a founding member of the National Committee for the Abolishment of the Poll Tax, which lobbied Congress unsuccessfully throughout the Roosevelt Administration, and of the Southern Conference on Human Welfare, which worked to build a political base for support in the south for New Deal reforms. Labeled by historian C. Vann Woodward "the most important white woman of the South in the civil rights movement," Mrs. Durr was a friend and active supporter of the Reverend Martin Luther King.

GERALD R. FORD, Thirty-eighth President of the United States, was first elected to the U.S. House of Representatives in 1948. During his thirteen terms in the House, he became the ranking Republican on the Appropriations Committee's powerful Subcommittee on Defense Department Appropriations and was considered an expert in the field. In 1963 he was elected Chairman of the House Republican Conference, and in 1965 he became House Minority Leader. He also served as a member of the Warren Commission, which investigated the assassination of President John F. Kennedy. He became Vice-President under Richard Nixon in 1973, succeeding to the Presidency following Mr. Nixon's resignation on August 9, 1974. His autobiography, *A Time to Heal*, was published in 1979.

FRANK B. FREIDEL, an internationally known Roosevelt historian, has been the Bullitt Professor of American History at the University of Washington since 1981. He taught for over twenty-five years at Harvard University, where he was the Charles Warren Professor of American History.

Dr. Freidel has written extensively on the Roosevelt Presidency, including such books as *FDR: The Ordeal* (1954); *Roosevelt: The Triumph* (1956); *FDR and the South* (1966); and *Roosevelt: Launching the New Deal* (1973). He also edited a series entitled *Franklin D. Roosevelt and the Era of the New Deal*.

JOHN KENNETH GALBRAITH is the Paul M. Warburg Professor of Economics Emeritus at Harvard University. Dr. Galbraith was Deputy Administrator of the Office of Price Administration in the early 1940s and principally organized the wartime system of price control, which he headed until 1943. He was awarded the Medal of Freedom by President Harry S. Truman.

An early supporter of John F. Kennedy, Dr. Galbraith was Chairman of the Economic Advisory Committee of the Democratic Advisory Council from 1956 to 1960 and served on Kennedy's 1960 convention staff. He was the U.S. Ambassador to India from 1961 to 1963.

A former editor of *Fortune* magazine, Dr. Galbraith has written many books, his most recent being his memoirs, *A Life in Our Times*. Other well-known works include *The Affluent Society*, *The New Industrial State*, and *The Age of Uncertainty*.

JOHN HOUSEMAN, well-known actor and director, was a beneficiary of the New Deal's Works Projects Administration. Employed under the WPA's Federal Arts Project, Mr. Houseman cofounded the Mercury Theater, which produced a variety of highly successful plays during the Depression and launched the careers of many now-famous performers. His own career has included not only acting, directing, and producing plays, operas, and motion pictures, but also teaching drama at such institutions as the Juilliard School in New York, Vassar College, the University of California at Los Angeles, and the University of South Carolina. Mr. Houseman won an Oscar for his performance in *The Paper Chase* in 1974.

MRS. LYNDON BAINES JOHNSON is perhaps best known for her support of environmental projects, an interest that began during her White House years. Her current activities in that area include serving as a member of the Advisory Council of National Parks, Historic Sites, Buildings, and Monuments; as a Trustee for the National Geographic Society; and as Cochairman of the National Wildflower Research Center near Austin, which she created in December 1982.

Mrs. Johnson is also actively involved in the activities of The University of Texas at Austin. In addition to serving on special committees and commissions of the University, she is a life member of its Ex-Students Association and served a six-year term as a member of the UT System Board of Regents. She also devotes much time supporting the activities of the Lyndon B. Johnson Presidential Library and Museum and the LBJ School of Public Affairs on the University of Texas campus.

VERNON E. JORDAN, JR., is a partner in the law firm of Akin, Gump, Strauss, Hauer, and Feld in Washington, D.C. He has served as President of the National Urban League, as Executive Director of the United Negro College Fund, and as a member of numerous national boards, commissions, and councils, including the Presidential Clemency Board and the Advisory Council on Social Security. A leader in the area of voluntarism and minority rights, he has received many awards in recognition of his accomplishments, including the prestigious Alexis de Tocqueville Award of the United Way of America. Mr. Jordan has authored a weekly newspaper column which appeared in over three-hundred newspapers and has been a frequent guest on major television broadcasts, including "Meet the Press," "Issues and Answers," and "Face the Nation."

W. PAGE KEETON, considered one of the nation's foremost authorities on torts, served for twenty-five years (1949-74) as dean of the University of Texas Law School, where he continues to teach and to hold the endowed W. Page Keeton Professorship in Law of Torts.

From 1942 to 1945, he served as counsel in several divisions of the U.S. Office of Price Administration and as Assistant General Counsel for the Petroleum Administration of War. Later, he was a member of President Lyndon B. Johnson's Advisory Committee on Labor Management Policy (1966-68), a member of the Texas Constitutional Revision Commission, and Chairman of a State Bar committee that recommended reforms in the Texas Penal Code.

JACK F. KEMP has been U.S. Representative (Republican) from New York since 1971. Prior to entering the political arena, he was a professional football player for thirteen years. During that period he was named American Football League Player of the Year (1965), All-AFL Quarterback, and winner of the National Football Hall of Fame Award.

In 1967, Mr. Kemp served as Special Assistant to the Governor of California, and in 1969, he was Special Assistant Chairman of the Republican National Committee. He currently is a member of the House Appropriations Committee and the Subcommittee on Defense.

LEON H. KEYSERLING began his career as an economic adviser in the 1930s. As assistant to U.S. Senator Robert Wagner and chief consultant to the Senate Committee on Banking and Currency, he was a major contributor to such legislation as the National Recovery Act of 1933, the National Labor Relations Act of 1935, and the U.S. Housing Act of 1937. Mr. Keyserling also held administrative posts with a number of housing agencies during the Roosevelt Presidency and was responsible for drafting Roosevelt's executive order creating the National Housing Agency, the forerunner of the Department of Housing and Urban Development (HUD). During the Truman Administration he was appointed to the first Council of Economic Advisers, serving as Vice-Chairman and then Chairman.

After leaving publice service Mr. Keyserling spent nearly twenty years in private practice as a consulting economist. Since 1971 he has been active in voluntary public service, including work with the Conference on Economic Progress, which he founded in 1954.

MARY DUBLIN KEYSERLING is a consulting economist in private practice in Washington, D.C. She is also a lecturer and writer on economics, welfare, and women's issues. Mrs. Keyserling has held many high-level economic posts during the past forty-five years, including Chief of the Research and Statistics Division in the Office of Civilian Defense, where she was an assistant to Mrs. Eleanor Roosevelt; Chief of the International Economic Analysis Division of the U.S. Department of Commerce; and Chief of the Liberated Areas Division of the Foreign Economics

Administration. President Johnson appointed her to serve in his Administration as Director of the Women's Bureau of the U.S. Department of Labor.

Mrs. Keyserling is presently President of the Clearinghouse on Women's Issues and is Chairperson of the National Consumers Committee for Research and Education. She continues to be active in numerous organizations related to consumers, women, health, and child welfare.

WILLIAM E. LEUCHTENBURG, one of the nation's foremost New Deal historians, is the DeWitt Clinton Professor at Columbia University and the William Rand Kenan Professor at the University of North Carolina at Chapel Hill. His best-known book, *Franklin D. Roosevelt and the New Deal* (1963), won the Francis Parkman Prize and the Bancroft Prize in 1964. Among the other volumes he has written or edited are *The New Deal and Global War* (1964), *Franklin D. Roosevelt: A Profile* (1967), *The New Deal: A Documentary History* (1968), and *A History of American Presidential Elections* (1971). A member of the faculty of Columbia University for over thirty years, Dr. Leuchtenburg has also been an adviser to the Social Security Administration since 1964 and serves on the Advisory Committee to the U.S. Senate Historical Office.

KATIE LOUCHHEIM was the first woman to be named Deputy Assistant Secretary of State, a position she held in the early 1960s. She has also been actively involved with the United Nations, serving as Deputy Director of Public Information for the U.N. Relief and Rehabilitation Administration during World War II and later as the U.S. Representative on the Executive Board of the U.N. Education, Scientific, and Cultural Organization (UNESCO). Other positions she has held are Director of Women's Activities and Vice-Chairman of the Democratic National Committee.

An accomplished writer, Mrs. Louchheim has published two volumes of poetry; her memoirs, *By the Political Sea*; and a recent volume entitled *Making of the New Deal: The Insiders Speak*.

CHARLES C. MCLAUGHLIN is Professor of History and American Studies at the American University in Washington, D.C. A member of the faculty since 1963, Dr. McLaughlin specializes in the study of Frederick Law Olmsted, a nineteenth-century American landscape architect. Since 1973 he has served as editor-in-chief of a project on the Frederick Law Olmsted Papers, which has produced two major volumes in recent years.

HARRY J. MIDDLETON, Director of the Lyndon Baines Johnson Library and Museum in Austin, served as White House Staff Assistant to President Johnson from 1967 to 1969. A former writer and media consultant, his publications include *Pax*, a novel, and *The Compact History of the Korean War*. He also was a reporter for the Associated Press in New York, News Editor of *Architectural Forum Magazine*, and writer and director of *The March of Time*.

CLARENCE M. MITCHELL, JR., a Baltimore attorney, served for twenty-eight years as Director of the Washington Bureau of the National Association for the Advancement of Colored People (NAACP). Prior to assuming the directorship in 1950, Mr. Mitchell served as NAACP's Labor Secretary and held several executive positions in offices of the federal government, including the Office of Production Management, the War Production Board, and the War Manpower Commission. He also worked on the staff of the Fair Employment Practices Committee and was a member of President Truman's Committee to Employ the Physically Handicapped. In recognition of his leadership in the area of minority rights, Mr. Mitchell has received many honors and awards, including the Presidential Medal of Freedom.

GEORGE H. NASH has been involved since 1975 in the preparation of a multivolume scholarly biography of Herbert Hoover, commissioned by the Hoover Presidential Library Association. Dr. Nash, who received his Ph.D. in American history from Harvard University, is a regular contributor to *National Review*, an editorial adviser to *Modern Age*, and associate editor of *American Journal*. He is the author of *The Conservative Intellectual Movement in America Since 1945*, published by Basic Books in 1976.

CLAUDE D. PEPPER, U.S. Representative from Florida's Third District, has served in both houses of the U.S. Congress. He was first elected to the Senate in 1936, serving there until 1950. During that period he was a member of the Senate Foreign Relations Committee (1937-50), Chairman of the Subcommittees on the Middle East and Wartime Health and Education, and Chairman of the Inter-oceanic Canal Committee. Mr. Pepper lost his bid for reelection in 1950, but in 1962 he was elected to the House of Representatives, where he continues to serve. During the 1970s he became well known for his legislative efforts on behalf of the nation's elderly, and he continues to serve as Chairman of the House Select Committee on Aging and the Subcommittee on Health and Long-Term Care.

ESTHER PETERSON began her long career in labor and consumer affairs in the 1930s, serving as Assistant Director of Education and then as Legislative Representative for the Amalgamated Clothing Workers. She later held high-level posts under three Presidents. John F. Kennedy appointed her Director of the Women's Bureau in the U.S. Department of Labor, as Assistant Secretary of Labor for Labor Standards, and as Executive Vice-Chairman of the President's Commission on the Status of Women, chaired by Eleanor Roosevelt. Under President Johnson she was the first Special Assistant to the President for Consumer Affairs and Chairman of the President's Commission on Consumer Interests. In the Carter Administration she again served as Special Assistant for Consumer Affairs, as well as Chairman of the Consumer Affairs Council, which President Carter created to ensure that consumers had a voice in federal policymaking and programs.

Ms. Peterson serves on the boards of directors of many consumer, educational, and civic organizations, and has received numerous awards, including the Presidential Medal of Freedom.

J. J. (JAKE) PICKLE has been U.S. Representative from the 10th District of Texas since 1964. As third-ranking Democrat on the House Ways and Means Committee, Congressman Pickle has been deeply involved in the economic and tax legislation that has dominated the Congress in recent years. As Chairman of the Subcommittee on Social Security, he has been a leader in the efforts to address the long-range financing problems of the system through reform legislation. Among his many other legislative contributions have been coauthorship of legislation opening up Individual Retirement Accounts to the general public, authorship of tax code amendments to reduce the inheritance tax on small farms and businesses, and introduction of legislation to aid cancer patients, balance the budget, and protect the environment.

JENNINGS RANDOLPH, U.S. Senator (Democrat) from West Virginia, is the only person now serving in Congress who was part of the first one-hundred days of the Roosevelt Administration. Elected to the House of Representatives in 1932, he served as Congressman for fourteen years and was elected Majority Whip during his tenure there.

In 1958 he was elected to the Senate and has served continuously since that time. As a member of the Senate Committee on Environment and Public Works throughout his twenty-six years in the Senate, he has sponsored many of the laws concerning air and water pollution control and highway and water resource development. Senator Randolph has also been the leading spokesman for and author of almost all legislation for disabled persons enacted during his career in the Congress.

CHARLES S. ROBB was elected Governor of Virginia in 1981, following four years of service as Lieutenant Governor. Active in government committee work, he has been Vice-Chairman of the Local Government Advisory Commission and Chairman of the Intergovernmental Affairs Committee. In addition, he has served as Chairman of the Virginia Forum on Education since 1978. Trained as an attorney, he was a member of the law firm of Williams, Connolly, and Califano before entering the public service.

Governor Robb is married to the former Lynda Bird Johnson, daughter of President and Mrs. Lyndon B. Johnson.

JAMES ROOSEVELT, eldest son of Franklin Roosevelt, was a six-term U.S. Congressman (Democrat) from California. He also served as U.S. Representative to the United Nations Economic and Social Council from 1965 to 1967. He currently is President of James Roosevelt and Company, a business consulting firm in Newport Beach, California.

Mr. Roosevelt's philanthropic activities have included serving as Vice-President of the Eleanor Roosevelt Cancer Foundation, as member of the Board of the Eleanor Roosevelt Institute, and as President of the National Committee for Research.

He is the author of several books, including *Affectionately, FDR; My Parents: A Differing View*; and *A Family Matter*.

ELSPETH ROSTOW, Dean of the Lyndon B. Johnson School of Public Affairs from 1977 to 1983, has been a member of the UT Austin faculty since 1969. A specialist in American diplomatic history and domestic politics, she has taught at a variety of institutions, including Barnard College, Sarah Lawrence College, the University of Zurich, the Salzburg Seminar in Austria, Massachusetts Institute of Technology, American University, and Georgetown University.

In addition to her many appointments and activities related to higher education, Mrs. Rostow has held numerous government appointments, including membership on President Carter's Commission for a National Agenda for the Eighties and on his Advisory Committee for Trade Negotiations.

JAMES H. ROWE began his long career as a legal adviser in the public sector during the Roosevelt Administration. In the 1930s he served as an attorney for the National Emergency Council, the Department of Labor, the Public Works Administration, and the Securities Exchange Commission. He also served as secretary to Supreme Court Justice Oliver Wendell Holmes and as assistant to both President Roosevelt and James Roosevelt. From 1941 to 1943 he was Assistant U.S. Attorney General and later served as technical adviser at the International Military Tribunal in Nuremberg.

Among the many positions Mr. Rowe held in later years were Commissioner of the Roosevelt Memorial Commission, Chairman of the Advisory Committee on Personnel for the Secretary of State, and Counsel to the Senate Majority Policy Committee.

(*The editor regrets to note that Mr. Rowe died in Washington, D.C., in June 1984.*)

WILLIAM RUSHER has been publisher of the *National Review* since 1957. A well-known conservative spokesman, he has appeared regularly on such programs as PBS's *The Advocates* and the "Face Off" feature of ABC's *Good Morning, America*. Mr. Rusher is also a prolific author, with a thrice-weekly syndicated column, "The Conservative Advocate," and a number of books to his name, including *The Making of the New Majority Party* and *How to Win Arguments*.

In the 1950s he served as Associate Counsel to the Senate Internal Security Subcommittee and in the late 1960s as Vice-Chairman of the American Conservative Union.

RICHARD TALLBOYS has been the British Consul General at the United Kingdom Consulate in Houston since 1980. Prior to that he held the rank of Lieutenant Commander in the Royal Australian Navy.

ESTHER VAN WAGONER TUFTY is the founder of the Tufty News Service, an organization primarily serving newspapers in her native Michigan. Ms. Tufty's numerous roles for the service, which was started in Washington, D.C. in 1935, have included working as managing editor, foreign correspondent, radio commentator, and Washington correspondent, covering every Presidency since the early days of Franklin Roosevelt's Administration. She also served as a war correspondent during World War II, the Korean War, and the Vietnam War.

WILLIAM S. WHITE, a Pulitzer prize-winning author, has written several books on U.S. congressional history and U.S. presidents. Included among those are *Majesty and Mischief: A Mixed Tribute to FDR* and *The Professional: Lyndon B. Johnson*. He has also been a contributing editor and regular essayist for *Harper's Magazine*.

A news reporter for many years, Mr. White was the war editor for the Associated Press during World War II, covering the D-Day invasion and participating in several Allied assault forces in Europe. He also served as Senate and chief Congressional correspondent for the *New York Times* and later wrote an internationally synidicated column.

In addition to many other honors, Mr. White is the recipient of the Presidential Medal of Freedom.

WILBUR J. COHEN, editor of the volume, has been a Professor at the LBJ School of Public Affairs since 1980. He began his long career in human services in 1934 when he went to Washington as research assistant to the Executive Director of President Roosevelt's Cabinet Committee on Economic Security, which drafted the original Social Security Act. In 1935 he joined the staff of the Social Security Board and subsequently was Assistant Director and then Director of its Division of Research and Statistics. Between 1961 and 1968 he served as Assistant Secretary, Under Secretary, and Secretary of Health, Education, and Welfare, the only person ever to hold all three positions. During that period he also served as chairman of President Kennedy's Task Force on Health and Social Security and President Johnson's Committees on Population and Family Planning and Mental Retardation.

In 1969, Mr. Cohen became Dean of the School of Education at the University of Michigan, a post he held until 1978. He has continued to be active in government and human services through appointments to federal committees and task forces. He was a member of President Jimmy Carter's Task Force on Education (1976), Chairman of Carter's National Commission on Unemployment Compensation (1978-80), and a member of the National Commission on Social Security (1979-81) by appointment of Speaker O'Neill.

INTRODUCTION

Franklin D. Roosevelt undoubtedly ranks among our three greatest Presidents. With Washington and Lincoln he was first in war and first in plans for peace in his time. Like Lincoln, he was intensely controversial during his Presidency. The only President to serve more than two terms, Roosevelt presided over vast changes which not only affected the lives of those who lived at the time, but basically changed the institutional structure of the nation for all time to come.

It was perhaps inevitable, therefore, that on the fiftieth anniversary of FDR's inauguration, an evaluation of the Roosevelt revolution and its legacy would be undertaken. The timing was all the more desirable since a considerable number of Roosevelt Administration participants and observers were still available in 1983 to discuss what actually took place and how they saw their efforts in retrospect.

In the half-century between the Roosevelt Administration and the evaluative conference, these participants had lived through not only World War II, the Korean War, and the Vietnam War, but the Republican Administrations of Eisenhower, Nixon, and Ford, the Democratic tenures of Truman, Kennedy, Johnson, and Carter, and the first phase of the Reagan Administration. Their involvement in these Administrations varied widely, giving them—as a group—a unique set of experiences and perspectives with which to view the Roosevelt legacy.

With these aspects in mind, I proposed to Elspeth Rostow, then Dean of the LBJ School of Public Affairs, that we bring together in Austin both some of the outstanding current historians of the New Deal period and the available surviving participants and observers. This idea was enthusiastically endorsed by Dean Rostow, Harry Middleton, Director of the LBJ Library and Museum, Peter Flawn, President of the University of Texas at Austin, and Mrs. Lyndon B. Johnson and the Johnson Foundation.

We shortly discovered that Professor Melvin Urofsky of Virginia Commonwealth University had independently been making arrangements for a seminar at which historians would present a series of scholarly papers on the New Deal. Professor Urofsky, Mr. Middleton, and I met to discuss our varied interests and decided to join forces in a common effort with the cooperation of the National Archives and the Roosevelt Library at Hyde Park. A more congenial, enthusiastic, and cooperative spirit could not be imagined. With the assistance of a broad-based University of Texas Advisory Committee, the enterprise became a full-scale nationwide event. A conference of two separate-but-related parts was held March 1-4, 1983, on the University of Texas campus. The first part consisted of presentations of scholarly papers on nine aspects of the New Deal, ranging from farm policy to women's rights. Following the working conference was the public symposium on which this volume is based. It is the hope of the editor and others associated with the conference that the published proceedings will be of value and interest to scholars and students, politicians and policymakers. The coordinating committee decided before the event that it would not be feasible to include an evaluation of international policy or of World War II, and therefore it limited the conference and its publication solely to domestic policies.

For myself, my interest in the conference derives from the historical fact that I was nineteen years old when FDR made his historic inaugural speech on March 4, 1933. I was an economics major at the University of Wisconsin in Madison. The economic depression of 1929 had devastated my parents' friends and business associates and had adversely affected the economic independence of my parents and my uncles and aunts. Yet by continued sacrifices, they were able to see me graduate from the University of Wisconsin in June 1934. Like others of my age I was attracted to the dynamism and experimentation of the Roosevelt Administration. The inaugural message had remained a ringing challenge: "There is nothing to fear but fear itself. . . . "

In early August 1934, as I was planning to resume my studies, I learned that my professor, Edwin E. Witte, had gone to Washington to be in charge of development of the "economic" security program. He had indicated to Professor Selig Perlman there might be a research position for me with him. A student friend, Walker H. Hill, was driving back home to Richmond, Virginia, and he was willing to allow me sole occupancy of the "rumble" seat of his car. I enthusiastically took advantage of his kind offer and within a few days I found myself in Washington, D.C.

FDR—on the advice of Frances Perkins, the Secretary of Labor, and Harry Hopkins, the Federal Emergency Relief Administrator—had established a Cabinet Committee on Economic Security to develop a specific program of social security. Professor Witte was selected as its Executive Director, primarily on the recommendation of Arthur J. Altmeyer, another Wisconsin appointee, who was the Assistant Secretary of Labor. So with my appointment to the Committee's staff, I innocently became part of a Wisconsin Contingent which was to play a significant role in the formulation, development, and expansion of the social security program over a fifty-year period.

Some of the historians, scholars, writers, and commentators at the conference were critical in their assessments of the New Deal. I do not contest the validity of their criticisms. I have, as a matter of fact, written many similar criticisms myself. But for those who were privileged to participate, impartial historical evaluation falls far short of expressing the excitement and personal challenge which the New Deal generated. Perfection in public policy was not achieved; the millenium was not reached, nor did the designers of the New Deal expect it to be reached. But the joy of being a party to a national reformation, a peaceful domestic revolution, making a dream into a working institution, forged bonds of friendship and collegiality between people from Wisconsin and Texas, between inhabitants of big cities and rural towns, between men and women, between whites and blacks, and between individuals from vastly different social and economic classes from all over the nation, and these bonds have endured for over half a century. It was a rare experience. Friendships were intensified and bureaucracy was minimized. And government was able to demonstrate its compassion for the needs of people.

Roosevelt can be and has been criticized in a number of ways. He made a number of errors both in domestic policy and in the conduct of the war. He failed to take advantage of opportunities to make basic changes in the economic structure. He was not a tidy administrator. He was not acutely sensitive to problems of race or ethnicity, although he gave opportunities to minorities and women which had important long-term consequences.

Yet, like Lincoln, he was hated intensely for the same reasons others loved and respected him, and for the reasons millions, including Ronald Reagan, voted for him on four occasions. His willingness to experiment and improvise, his self-confident air, his jaunty personality, and his ability to communicate with the rank and file of workers and farmers despite his patrician upbringing, all contributed to the strong support he evoked among a majority of voters and the critical opposition from a minority. Mrs. Roosevelt was an equally controversial figure, and her special role as First Lady in a changing social order deserves special treatment.

It is difficult to know where to begin a book about FDR and equally difficult to know where to end it. He remains a fascinating figure. Washington presided over a helter-skelter war with meager resources and the foundation of a great democratic Republic. Lincoln presided over our only episode of civil disobedience in which members of single families tragically fought on both sides of the war. Roosevelt presided over the efforts to deal with the worst economic catastrophe in American history and the most far-reaching war with the most devasting weapons in the history of the world up to that time. We were fortunate to have three such leaders at three of the most critical times in our history. It is the precious heritage we honor here when we try to disassemble the various parts which made up the Roosevelt whole. It must necessarily be an incomplete and an imperfect result. Perhaps on the hundredth anniversary of the New Deal in the year 2033, a more final assessment can be written.

Wilbur J. Cohen

THE NEW DEAL

FIFTY YEARS AFTER

A HISTORICAL ASSESSMENT

WELCOME

HARRY J. MIDDLETON
MRS. LYNDON B. JOHNSON

Middleton   Johnson

HARRY MIDDLETON: The name of Franklin D. Roosevelt will be repeated often during the proceedings in this auditorium. But at the opening of this phase of the symposium, I would like to invoke a brief reflection on the name of another President of the United States.

Lyndon Johnson, marked though he was by FDR, is not the subject of this conference, but his hand is upon it because what we are doing here is work that he shaped for this library which bears his name and houses the record of his own life's work. He had a large vision of the library, as in the years of his leadership he had had for the American society. He knew this would be a place in the tradition of the presidential libraries which had come before it, where scholars would study the records of the past and where the public would be able to reflect on events hopeful and tragic alike of a significant era in their national history. But he wanted more.

President Johnson established this series of national symposia. He lived to participate in the first two, which were close to his own concerns. They were on education and civil rights. As

President, Johnson had been an activist and no stranger to controversy, and he made no effort to hide or moderate either of those qualities when he spoke from this stage in the final months of his life.

He summed it all up in the civil rights symposium the month before he died when he advocated action to achieve equal justice even beyond those steps taken during his Presidency in the 1960s. He said on that occasion, "Some will respond with exclamations of shock and dismay. I can only hear such protests through ears attuned to listening to the language of evasion—unthinkable, impossible, never, never—but our challenge is, as it has always been, to make never now."

That was Johnson the activist. But he was also a realist. He saw the pendulum begin to swing the other way, and he instructed us in the virtues of contention. He made it clear that he wanted us to create a place where leaders of the time, representing all points of view, would come to discuss, to debate, and to illuminate issues of great concern to the American people.

In that spirit, there have been assembled here not only his supporters but also those who challenged his philosophy and opposed his programs and his actions. The result has been a decade of lively, often exciting, sometimes contentious, and I hope useful conferences culminating in this one. That is part of his legacy.

But he left us more than a legacy and a hope. He left us, also, a leader, whose own hope for this institution was as strong as his, the standards as demanding, the zeal every bit as high—but whose touch is considerably more gentle. President Johnson set us on the road. We have followed her the rest of the way.

It is my privilege now to invite her to this podium to extend all of you a welcome from all of us—Lady Bird Johnson.

MRS. LYNDON B. JOHNSON: Dear friends, this is where I came in. This is where so many of us in this room came in—the thirties, those vigorous days of our youth. Among us are friends from NYA, REA, all those alphabetic experiments of the New Deal. Among us also are students and others too young to have lived through it, but this is where so much that shaped your lives began as well. We will start now in this symposium to relive a slice of history in which we all, young and old, shared. For me, for all who were part of it, the Depression hit in a very personal way. There was an experience, a vignette, a memory that each of us still carries with us.

I was a student on this campus when that moment occurred. A letter from my daddy, country merchant and landowner back in Karnack, with a dollar bill in it, said, "Dear Daughter, I am sending you the last dollar from the cash register. We don't know when the banks will open." Times were hard and you could read it in the lines of letters and faces.

In 1934, when Lyndon, who was then secretary to a Congressman, took me to Washington as a bride, there was an upbeat in the air. I could feel the yeasty sense of doing that pervaded the Capital. Like so many young couples in Washington, we were swept up in the talk and the action—government in action. The bold young people that I was associated with thought we could roll up our sleeves and remake America. As Tommy Corcoran said, "the lights burned all night" in the offices.

But this symposium is designed as more than a memory or a celebration. It is intended as an assessment to explore where we have been as a nation and where we are going. Assembled here to help us in that adventure are those who were there when it was happening, scholars who have made a life study of the New Deal, correspondents who have reported it in all its facets, political leaders of both parties who have grappled with its meaning, and members of today's generation who inherit its fifty-year legacy.

What has endured? What should endure? I will be sitting eagerly on the front row during the next two days to hear the answers pursued and debated. I am so glad that pursuit and debate will take place here in this library in such distinguished company, so many of whom I have known and loved for so many years.

Rostow

Galbraith

Cohen

Durr

Keeton

Keyserling

Rowe

Tufty

White

Houseman

Cuneo

I

HOW IT ALL BEGAN

ELSPETH ROSTOW
JOHN KENNETH GALBRAITH
WILBUR J. COHEN
VIRGINIA FOSTER DURR
W. PAGE KEETON
LEON H. KEYSERLING
JAMES H. ROWE, JR.
ESTHER VAN WAGONER TUFTY
WILLIAM S. WHITE
JOHN HOUSEMAN
ERNEST L. CUNEO

INTRODUCTION OF SPEAKER

ELSPETH ROSTOW: It is my pleasant task to introduce the next speaker. I would like to begin by discussing the set within which he belongs. This is the set of academics who not only have been participants in government but have given some themes and advice and counsel to Presidents. In one sense, you can judge a President by the quality of the information that he seeks as well as by the use that he makes of it. In other words, it's a measure of his leadership to select people who can give him the range of options from which he—and I must say "he" so far—may select the course of action for the period of history in which he is in office.

It's interesting to look at the twentieth century, because it's really only since the 1930s that we've begun to see academics playing significant roles as presidential advisers, as people in government. Look, for example, at McKinley and Mark Hanna. Whatever Mr. Hanna's virtues, he would not have gotten tenure. Later on, Colonel House gave interesting suggestions to Woodrow Wilson, but, of course, President Wilson, himself a Ph.D., didn't really feel the need of consulting with other colleagues, which is occasionally an academic deformation.

In the thirties, however, the condition of both the economy and the political structure suggested the appropriateness, or at least the possibility, of bringing from universities people who would form a part of the advice structure for a President in need of precisely that kind of counsel.

I wondered for a moment why I'd never read an article about professors in government, but then I realized what the acronym would be and I understood thoroughly. Let's call them academics, since that sounds better. The concept of seeking information from the professions began in the mind of Franklin Roosevelt before he went to Washington. While he was in Albany as Governor of New York, he began to consult with professors to an extent unusual at that time. He drew in large part, but not exclusively, from Columbia, and later on he widened his net. His pool included economists, political scientists, lawyers, and ultimately a social worker. From this array of information he was then able to select the options which he felt the country needed. It's therefore wholly appropriate in an academic institution to welcome people who have played a part in this important continuum between the campus and the White House.

The first speaker in this program has played a very significant role. The only thing that I shall say at the outset is that the sheet of information which came from Mr. Galbraith's office is totally unlike its subject. It has three characteristics. It is short, it is modest, and it is dull. So I shan't use it.

Even before the Kennedy Administration came to power, John Kenneth Galbraith played a role in this country that is worth noting. Not only had he been in the Office of Price Administration during World War II, where he played a significant policy-forming role; not only had he in the 1950s written *American Capitalism: The Concept of Countervailing Power* and the more widely noted *Affluent Society*, which shaped the way we perceived our world; but he also, of course, by adorning the Harvard campus, had been a part of that select area from which all but my husband, who comes from Yale, would say the best ideas emanate.

Mr. Galbraith at this stage became so well known that Arthur Schlesinger tells us in *The Thousand Days* that that quintessential member of the Eastern Establishment, Bob Lovett, voted for Richard Nixon out of fear of Galbraith. Schlesinger does not elaborate, but we had then in the towering presence of Ken Galbraith a figure with a remarkable mind, trained in economics but straying into the adjacent fields of politics and public policy, with the important ability to affect American attitudes and American beliefs.

Those economists whose books did not sell looked at Ken Galbraith with special eyes, because his did and do. I will not list them to you, but they have been as important as any set of economic documents in determining the way we regard our post-industrial society, the way we look at liberalism, and certainly the way we consider economic issues. Not averse to discussing these matters in public, before a camera, and doing so always with a felicity of style which alas is not wholly characteristic of the economic fraternity, he has long been a figure whose ideas, whether we agree with them or not, make us feel that we have been the better for having had him put them before us.

The Paul M. Warburg Professor of Economics Emeritus, Ken

Galbraith, then, is in every way the appropriate person to look over the span of American history in which he has been so vigorous a participant from the late thirties down to the present. He has been a spokesman. He has been a critic. He has been an advocate. He has been everything but silent, and his absence of silence has been a great gift to us all.

LOOKING BACK: ROOSEVELT'S NEW DEAL IN THE MAKING

JOHN KENNETH GALBRAITH

The somber subject which you have given me today is the role of Franklin D. Roosevelt in our history. That he was, and preeminently, the dominant political figure of this century will not be doubted, nor the reasons subject to serious dispute. It was the Roosevelt fate and fortune to face the two great tragedies of the time and also to guide its greatest social achievement. The tragedies were, of course, the Second World War and the Great Depression.

As to the bearing of these two events on the Roosevelt transcendence, I think few will quarrel. The world emerged better and in some ways stronger from both. We do not know in either case the disasters that might have been. Nor will there be much disagreement on the Roosevelt achievement. It was Franklin D. Roosevelt who in the United States led the great transition in modern capitalism—the transition from an economic and social system in which participants were expected to bear the cost of their own helplessness and their own misfortune, earned or unearned, to a system in which a compassionate protection tempered the inherent hardships and cruelties of what is still, by some, called the free enterprise system. Unemployment compensation, old age pensions, lower cost housing, varied support to agriculture, the National Youth Administration, employment opportunity, and much more came together to comprise this change, what collectively has been termed the New Deal and might be termed the Roosevelt Revolution.

The Roosevelt Revolution, the New Deal, to this day is both celebrated and not quite forgiven. The poor are still thought by the stern to be unduly favored, with resulting moral damage. Under free enterprise, men and women, and also children, are meant to suffer. That suffering is essential as an incentive.

No one would be more pleased than Franklin D. Roosevelt at the success of the Roosevelt Revolution, or less surprised at the deeply theological resistance it continues to engender. But that the Depression, the war, and the great economic and social transformation were central to the making of the Age of Roosevelt and the New Deal will, as I have said, be generally accepted. Historians can often unite even on the obvious. But what remains sharply in debate are the qualities of mind and personality that brought FDR, faced with such tragedy and such challenge, to such eminence.

Never did history have so dense a pace as between 1932 and 1945. There was enough in those years to have overthrown a lesser man a dozen times. What allowed one leader so to dominate such a time? There is a flaw, however reluctantly it may be conceded, in the testimony of anyone who was there. That is because if love and loyalty have a blinding effect, surely they had it in the case of Roosevelt.

I have told it before. The word of FDR's death which reached me on that April evening in 1945 brought a sense of trauma that I had never previously experienced in my life. There had been a faith, an affection, and a commitment that had seemed forever. Never in the preceding twelve years had it occurred to me that a President might be wrong, a view that I have since revised.

Were a Roosevelt decision or action in conflict with my earlier views, I was easily able to make the requisite adjustment so as to agree with Roosevelt, and I promptly did so. And so it was with the others who proudly called themselves Roosevelt men. Thus my warning against too easily accepting us as witnesses. But as I've just said, we are far, far better in our judgment of modern Presidents. The ability to ensure loyalty, the compelling sweep of the Roosevelt personality, were certainly important in the Roosevelt achievement. Of this perhaps enough has been said. Important, too, was the Roosevelt joy in the battle, and here a word might be added.

There are politicians who evade battle. There are those who invite it. The one who invites it, as did FDR, earns a loyalty from his followers not given to those politicians whose instinct is to accommodation, appeasement, and retreat. That is partly because there is pleasure in the contest. It is also because there is no danger that the retreat or the surrender will leave the soldiers leaderless and exposed.

This is not, of course, to say that Roosevelt never yielded. He was a master, as of much else, of the tactical withdrawal, but he never retreated because he was averse to the battle, to the conflict. He never yielded because he sought to be loved by his enemies.

In consequence, one of the Roosevelt legacies is the adversary tradition in American social and economic policy. The feeling of American business that government is inherently and intrinsically inimical is wrong, and in lesser measure the reverse is wrong. And everyone will think this a good legacy. On more matters than not, government and business interests have complementary roles.

Nor in the longer, deeper view was the conflict real. The Roosevelt Revolution, properly viewed, was deeply conservative. It came about in the interest of preserving the social tranquility, the sense of belonging without which capitalism would not have survived, and still will not survive. It protected values and institutions which were then very much at risk. But in the other industrial lands, the softening of the edges of capitalism and the transition to the welfare state were accomplished far more harmoniously than in the United States. In many of the industrial countries it is not quite clear who is responsible for this great change.

There is, however, no similar doubt in our case. Perhaps—who can say—it may all have come about here more peacefully, with less enduring strain on the political fabric. I do believe that something must be attributed to Roosevelt's delight in his enemies, to his commitment to the ancient injunction that one should not only comfort the afflicted, but one should also afflict the comfortable.

Certainly, this attitude added to the joy of all who were there. With what pleasure we made the President's enemies our own. How deeply we scorned those among us who were thought to have an instinct to appease. How unpleasant we must have been as people with whom to do business.

There is a myth cultivated by Walter Lippmann, among others, that Roosevelt was a man of words, not of thought. That it was his practice to air ideas liberally, to test them on audiences, casual and otherwise, is certainly not in doubt, and since he did this, many in consequence came away in deep alarm as to the direction in which the President's mind seemed to be running.

But the Roosevelt performance was distinctly different. Ideas were there, linked to intensely practical, powerfully relevant action. There were diverse thoughts on the causes of the prevailing farm crisis. His solution was to provide the farmers with cheap loans and organize them to produce less for higher prices. Whatever the reasons for unemployment, the obvious answer was for the government to provide jobs through the Public and Civil Works Administrations.

The National Recovery Act, the NRA, much belabored by economists then and ever since, recognized a basic characteristic of modern capitalism. This is a matter of high importance. It recognized that wages and prices in the modern economy have an interacting dynamic—that prices can shove down wages, that lower wages and reduced purchasing power can force yet further reductions, and that one can have a cumulative spiral of inflation. The opposing dynamic—wages pressing up prices, prices pulling up wages, something that we have recognized in more modern times—is also a cause of inflation, as we know today, or should.

Then, as now, there was a strong practical case for direct action to arrest this malign process, whether it is driving prices down or whether it is driving prices up. There was a practical case for the NRA. Unemployment compensation, old age pensions, and public housing were also eminently relevant to the problems they addressed.

The mobilization of the American economy in World War II was the most successful exercise in economic management in modern times—huge increases in production and no net reduction in aggregate civilian consumption, all with no appreciable inflation. On none of these matters was the President lacking in alternative proposals. Elaborate designs that substituted pretense and rhetoric for real solutions were eminently available. I don't suggest that FDR's ability to link ideas to effective action was infallible. In 1933, he, like more recent Presidents, was briefly attracted to the magic of the Monetarists, to the notion that the economy could be regulated in all its complexity by monetary witchcraft. His unfortunate guide in those days was Professor G. F. Warren, the forerunner of my good friend Professor Milton Friedman.

But in this case, in brilliant contrast to his successors, Franklin D. Roosevelt quickly relented, although one notices that other Presidents have also wisely relented. Roosevelt was indeed a man of many ideas, but it was his genius in the end to select those that were most relevant to a firm and useful result.

Those who would agree, at least in part, on the effect of some individual Roosevelt measures have another comment. They concede that these measures were a necessary response to diverse need. They insist, however, that the President was incapable of envisaging and embracing a comprehensive and internally consistent design, that he had no all-inclusive theory of the State, the economy, and the social order.

I believe this to be true, and it is something, I suggest, that no one can regret. Those scholars and politicians who seek such an overall design are almost always more impressive in oratory than they are in action, and they can be callous and cool as they pursue their plan or await its effects. Coolidge and Hoover had such a design—to leave the economy and all of its complexity to the ultimately benign operation of laissez faire. Those who suffer in the interim are the natural cost of the larger benefit. There is a similar plan in the minds of those who now speak so confidently of the miracle of the market, the pervasive wickedness of public regulation, and the generally inimical character of the modern welfare state.

There is no more powerful lesson in the twentieth century than the suffering that can be imposed right and also left by those who were captured by a comprehensive design for social and economic policy. We remember and celebrate Roosevelt because, mercifully, he was exempt from any cruel and confining theory. He moved from the needed result to the relevant action precisely because he was unencumbered by ideological constraint. That, no doubt, is another way of saying that Franklin D. Roosevelt was a superbly practical man.

The willingness to adapt to change, to act, was at the basis of Roosevelt's success as a political leader and of his hold on the American people and through them on the Congress. No one can doubt the Roosevelt virtuosity in speech, in dealing with the press, and above all in communicating on the radio, but none of this talent would have survived and served for those twelve intense years had it not been associated with concrete action and visible results.

We hear much in these days of the compelling television personality, the politician who has mastered this medium, allowing him to persuade workers, women, blacks, and the poor contrary to the viewer's need, interest, or fortune. I doubt that such a triumph of personality is truly possible. I would suggest that FDR's mastery of the radio and the fireside chat would not very long have survived the discovery that these stirring words were a disguise for social neglect and inaction.

Yet another source of the Roosevelt magic was his ability to extend a sense of community—a community not confined by national frontiers, and one to which all men and women of good will and good purpose could believe they belonged. When the President spoke of his commitment to economic betterment and justice, of his resistance to the repressive world of the dictators, and of his hope for a future in which the young would not face periodic slaughter and in which death would not be a statistic, he did not speak as a leader to followers, not even as a President to his people. He spoke as a participant to fellow participants. He spoke as one involved in an effort in which all had a part. It was this sense of a common effort with the President, of membership in a common community, to which people everywhere responded.

That the feeling was strongest here in the United States, none can doubt. Those who stood outside and who saw it as a threat to the economic and social eminence which had once been their more or less exclusive possession deeply resented it. They could not resist, because they could not get along. Once again, one sees Roosevelt's debt to his opposition.

But this sense of community went far beyond the actual boundaries of the United States. I saw it in my Canadian family. My father, in the more forthright language of the United States, would have been called a political boss. In Canada, he was merely the permanent leader of the Liberal Party in the Ontario Riding of West Elgin.

As a Canadian, he maintained his political commitment to Sir Wilfrid Laurier and then to William L. Mackenzie King, but his moral commitment in all his later years was to Franklin D. Roosevelt. And so it was with our neighbors. That stretch of Ontario reaches down between the lakes to Detroit, and each autumn after the crops were in, the younger members of the community went to Detroit, where they found work with General Motors or the Bridge Body Plant. Their commitment to Roosevelt was no passive phase. It included voting for him after they got to Detroit. They were given the names of the recently dead and went to the polls accordingly.

I remember asking a young contemporary about that practice,

because I had perhaps an unnatural sense of purity in these matters, and I was told indignantly that the man who had just died would have wanted that to happen.

Roosevelt extended the sense of being part of his community to Latin America. It was the essence of his avowal of the policy of the Good Neighbor. He extended it to Britain, most notably in those months when she stood alone, and on to distant India, where the commitment to Indian nationhood causes his name, as I personally can attest, to be revered there to this day.

It is the Roosevelt legacy that we all belong, without exception, to a yet larger commonwealth. In this larger community, there is a general concern for the economic well-being of all people and for the reality of social participation and social justice. Beyond this, there needs to be a commitment to the negotiation, conciliation, and peaceful resolution of national differences. Let this include our commitment as a world community to the problem of modern weaponry and getting this hideous prospect under control.

I end my remarks with a special plea that we have a sense of individual, personally expressed responsibility for ending the legacy that led to the tragedy of Hiroshima and Nagasaki. This is a legacy of the Roosevelt years to which we must address ourselves, for it is one on which our survival depends.

INTRODUCTION OF PANEL CHAIRMAN

ELSPETH ROSTOW: We turn now to a panel of equally talented and equally informed participants in the early period of the New Deal.

In order to introduce this part of the program, I will turn to another man who has been active in government, but who is also an academic. Wilbur Cohen is associated primarily with three academic institutions: Wisconsin, to which he returned and from which he has received an honorary degree; Michigan, where he became Professor in 1955 and where later he was Dean of Education and also Professor; and now The University of Texas, where he occupies the Sid Richardson Chair in the Lyndon B. Johnson School of Public Affairs.

Throughout his career, Wilbur Cohen has had a commitment to the field of human services, human welfare, and human rights. This has been indicated by the kinds of books and articles that he's written and the task forces and commissions that Presidents have appointed him to, and on which he has served admirably and effectively.

He is the only person who has occupied all three levels of Assistant Secretary, Under Secretary, and Secretary of HEW; and since the name of the agency has now been changed, he will remain in history as the only person who has occupied all three of these ranks.

In the course of these many activities, Professor Cohen has had time not only to become a friend of those in power, but to earn the respect of those who knew him from the very beginning on. He may take a strong position, and frequently does, but in addition to having a very effective speaking style, he can listen. And that is one of the characteristics of academics in government that is most highly prized. He can listen and he can learn, as well as teach.

It is, therefore, from another in-and-outer in government to an academic who has been influential over a span of roughly fifty years and whose voice is still heard, that I turn the direction of the panel.

PANEL PRESENTATIONS

WILBUR COHEN, CHAIR: The purpose of this panel is to present a subjective—even personal—view of the New Deal and the Roosevelt years through the eyes of individuals who were actually there.

For myself, I was nineteen years old in 1932 during the presidential campaign, a young student at the University of Wisconsin and a product of the La Follette progressivism of that time. During that campaign of 1932 we were not enchanted at all by Franklin D. Roosevelt. Those of us who heard him talk about balancing the budget and other such "suspicious" ideas were not attracted to him as a candidate in the later part of 1932. But his inaugural speech of March 4, 1933, electrified the young student body of which I was a member. Today we use the term charisma, but at that time Franklin D. Roosevelt's "We have nothing to fear but fear itself" speech became a new force in the political structure and made many of us eager to graduate and rush to Washington to work with the new Administration.

On my first job there, I earned $125 a month. My real income has never been larger in the ensuing fifty years. It was a stimulating time of associating with young people attracted to Franklin D. Roosevelt's dynamism, his willingness to experiment. That year of '34-35 remains in my own mind as one of the most thrilling times of my life.

I might add that many of those people I still write to and meet with nearly fifty years later. They have remained war buddies, I might say, in that we worked together in a common cause far beyond our individual abilities and far beyond our original conceptions. We were attached to something we thought was so much greater and so much more significant than our individual selves that we were propelled into a movement that has had a lifetime impact for each of us.

In my own case, helping to deal with the Social Security Program and the Unemployment Insurance Program has represented a lifetime effort, because succeeding Presidents that I have worked for inevitably said when they saw me, "Well, now, what would Franklin D. Roosevelt want to do if he were still alive to complete what he wasn't able to complete?" And I would say, "Well, he wanted to improve Social Security. He wanted a national health insurance program. He certainly wanted Medicare. He wanted a better unemployment insurance system." And those rather radical ideas of the twenties became accepted ideas of not only the thirties but later the forties, the fifties, the sixties, and even today.

In the discussion that follows, I hope the young people in the audience will get some sense of the contributions of individuals who have actually participated in the policy formulation process. I want them to see that institutions become realities through human beings, human beings with great abilities who also have certain limitations which we have to recognize.

VIRGINIA DURR: When I went to Washington in 1933, I went because my husband, Clifford Durr, was asked by my brother-in-law, Hubert Black, to come up and help save the banks. The banks were all shut up, and they wanted a lot of young lawyers to come and help open them. They called him up and asked if he would come and stay for six weeks or two months or so.

At the end of six weeks or two months he called me up (I was at home with the baby), and he said, "It's going to take longer than this to open the banks—you'd better come up." So we came up and stayed at the Virginia Episcopal Theological Seminary for the summer. At that time, 12 percent of the voting population of Virginia voted. Voting in Virginia was the most difficult thing you can possibly imagine. You had to go through the most intricate sort of registration, where you couldn't find the registrar, and when you did he didn't have a pen, and he'd forgotten the ink, and the register book had been lost, and if you ever got through that hurdle, then you had to go down to the Fairfax County Courthouse and you had to pay your poll tax, but you not only had to pay your present poll tax, you had to pay your poll tax for two years back, and that would come to four-fifty. Well, you may think that that four dollars and fifty cents was a very minor matter, but in those days it was a great deal of money. Four dollars and fifty cents was a tremendous amount of money to pay to be able to vote, and the difficulties of the voting process were absolutely impassable, unless you were very bright and unless you spent a great deal of time and energy.

So I decided that I would try to join something in the New Deal that was working on this particular problem. That turned out to be the Women's Division of the Democratic National Committee, headed at that time by Dorothy McAlister and May Thompson Evans. But we also had the advantage of having among us Mrs. Roosevelt, who was our great friend and our great leader, and Mrs. Mary McCloud Bethune.

So we in the Women's Division began a struggle within the Democratic Party to get the right to vote for the southern women. Now, as you remember, after the Civil War, the black men were given the right to vote, but neither the white women nor the black women were given the right to vote. And of course, when the Suffragette Amendment was passed, my home state of Alabama never ratified it. So the women of Alabama, black and white, were almost totally disenfranchised.

I grew up in an atmosphere in which it was considered to be rather bad taste to like to vote. I remember one of the Suffragette leaders lived near us, and she would pass by quite often on her mission back and forth in the streetcar. My mother would say, "I think she is really a beautiful and charming woman, but she does this because she likes men." And that was the general consensus about the women that got into politics. They did it because they liked men. In fact, the whole southern society, as far as women were concerned, was based purely on your attractions, and if you didn't have any, you had a pretty hard time.

Well, I hate to tell you, but at the age of fifteen and sixteen, I was too tall, I was too thin, I was nearsighted, I couldn't dance, and I was scared to death of boys, so you can imagine I was not a great belle. But I never thought about getting into anything, because nobody offered me anything, except marriage.

Finally, my husband, whom I wish I could talk about, came and rescued me and married me and took me up to Washington. I got into the fight against the poll tax, and we were doing absolutely wonderfully. We were getting committees started in all the southern states, and at that time, you must remember the southerners controlled the Congress completely. Howard Ward Smith was the head of the Rules Committee. Pat Harrison and the whole southern contingent were in control of the Congress, and they didn't like the idea of us trying to get rid of the poll tax and get the people to vote. So they sent the head of the Democratic Party, Jim Farley. He was a great big fat man, and he had a very red face, and he was an Irishman. And he just walked into the office, and there was May Thompson Evans, Dorothy McAlister, Mrs. Bethune, and I. Mrs. Roosevelt didn't happen to be there at the time. And he said, "Ladies, you've got to stop this." And we said, "Stop what?" And he said, "You've got to stop the fight against the poll tax." And we said, "Well, why should we do it?" And he said, "Because the southern Senators and the southern Congressmen don't like it. They think that if you go this far about the women, that you're bound to get the blacks into it."

Well, for the first time in my life I realized that the blacks were disenfranchised completely, and I was disenfranchised, and the poor whites were disenfranchised. This all dated back to the disenfranchisement revisions in 1901. So we had to go out and make a committee, a special committee outside of the Democratic Party, to try to get the vote for the South.

Bless God, oh, hallelujah! We found one brave southerner that would introduce a bill in the House, and his name was Maury Maverick, and he came from Austin, Texas. He introduced the bill into the House, and another Texan named Hatton Sumners sat on it for months and months and months and months and months, so we finally had to get it out on petition.

We got it through the House. We went up to the Senate, and another brave southerner who's going to be here tomorrow and who is a dear and beloved friend, Claude Pepper, introduced it in the Senate. Now, that was a very brave thing for him to do.

They had gotten rid of the poll tax in Florida by state action, so he wasn't quite as much in danger as somebody else would be, but he introduced it in the Senate, and it was filibustered. Well, it was filibustered year after year after year. We would sign it out of the House, it was filibustered in the Senate, and the South still didn't vote.

By that time I had met Lady Bird and Lyndon Johnson, and Lyndon was, as you know, Mr. Roosevelt's pet. He was his pet New Dealer, and he had a great deal of influence in the House. He was ten years younger than I was, so I felt like I could lecture him with a good deal of authority, and I did. I told him it was just disgraceful that he wouldn't vote for the anti-poll-tax bill and that I thought he was not acting right at all, and every time I saw him I just gave him a long lecture about it. And Lyndon said, "Honey, look, we ain't got the votes. I'm sorry, but," he said, "we haven't got the votes." He said, "I will promise you on my word of honor that when we get the votes, I will pass that bill." He did it thirty years later, in 1965. Lyndon Johnson passed the bill. He freed the South. He prevented, I think, a civil war. I think he was a second Lincoln in the fact he freed the South without any real bloodshed. And all I can say is, as I said to Lyndon when I called him up after he made that wonderful speech in the House when the bill was passed, "Free at last, free at last. Thank God almighty I am free at last."

PAGE KEETON: As Mrs. Johnson observed, the Depression was real to many of us during that period. I got my law license in 1931, and I doubt if many lawyers were included in the unemployment statistics because they were engaged in the law practice, allegedly. But there weren't many paying clients coming through the doors during that time, and I was fortunate enough to get an appointment to the University of Texas faculty one year after graduation from law school. But I think I have probably been the only one ever appointed to the law faculty who was retained and yet was cut in salary the second year after my appointment.

In FDR's nomination acceptance speech, we all remember that statement that proved to be both important and truthful: "I pledge you and I pledge myself to a New Deal for the American people." From the perspective of a lawyer, the New Deal permanently altered the role and function of the federal government in our so-called free society.

I say this because it led to two innovative actions on the part of the federal government. In the first place, the New Deal encompassed a commitment to the notion that the federal government could and should play a significant role in economic affairs. It need not simply stand by while the marketplace and free enterprise correct any imbalances and difficulties and injustices that exist. This concept was quite different from the Hoover Administration's idea that private enterprise and the marketplace would eventually right itself, if given time to do so.

In the second place, the New Deal committed the federal government to the notion of welfare for the needy. Our social welfare system was born. The launching of the welfare or the Social Security program in 1935 ended a period of reliance on the policies and practices of business to cure the evils of the competitive free market system. So I would say that, since the

New Deal, through trial and error, we no longer have free enterprise. What we have is regulated private enterprise that is competitive and not monopolistic, and I think we have been proving that in the long run this is the best system of all.

One of the characteristics of the New Deal was a willingness to experiment. It never did seem to me that that was a comprehensive policy, but there was a willingness to experiment, to try and do something about the situation that we were in.

One other point about the law. I think the New Deal was responsible for a revolution in constitutional law. It had a hard time coming about—FDR lost some battles along the way with the Supreme Court—but it came about nevertheless.

There were three ideas about the Constitution and the law that tended to interfere with New Deal efforts. One was that the federal government was a government of limited power—it had few delegated powers in the Constitution, and the rest went to the states. So the federal government had never been involved in welfare, and there was a great constitutional question, a legal question, as to whether welfare should be attempted at all by the federal government.

Another idea that created problems was the doctrine of separation of powers. The National Recovery Act was in trouble from the outset because of the notion that the Legislature could not delegate legislative power to the Executive. That doesn't bother us anymore. The Legislature, Congress, delegates to the Executive Branch all kinds of power now and it's always constitutional.

The third area of constitutional law that created problems for the New Deal related to the liberty of people to carry on their economic affairs without interference from the government. There was a strong and deep-seated conviction that governmental policy in economic affairs should be one of noninterference, and I might say that the law and the interpretation of the Constitution lent a good deal of support to that position.

But, the point to remember is that FDR was experimenting with new ideas and was committed to the notion that progress is worth the risks.

LEON KEYSERLING: My friends, I find it a little hard to talk here today, because I feel there is a miasma of academic misinformation about the New Deal and not enough time to set things straight. Now, if I had the time, I would make two points, both relating to my real interest in the New Deal, because I've been working for the New Deal for fifty years.

Our great America is now in a terrible condition. If you count it right, sixty million people are suffering directly the injustice and the indignity and the misery of unemployment. We are threatened with a tiny little recovery that will merely be an abortive succession to several periods of stagnation-recession, each getting worse. We are threatened with changes in tax laws and in spending laws which feed the fattened steer and starve the lean. We are threatened with political efforts to show that our troubles of today, which are really due to repudiation of the New Deal, were caused by what Franklin Roosevelt did fifty years ago and what Harry Truman did thirty years ago and what Lyndon Johnson did in the Great Society.

Let me digress here and tell about an experience I had when I first began to work in the New Deal and was awarding the first three housing projects under the new Slum Clearance and Low Rent Housing Program. One of them went to New York City, one of them went to New Orleans, both of which were understandable, and the third one went to Austin, Texas, all at the same time.

Well, it was desirable to award a project to a small southern town, but there were hundreds of thousands of small southern towns. Why Austin? The reason was very simple. There was a first-term Congressman who was by my office every other day, and that was why Austin got a project. And not only that, he called me up the day after the project was awarded and said, "Lady Bird and I would like you to have a drink with us. We want Austin to be announced first." I said, "Why should Austin be announced first?" He said, "Well, it's first in the alphabet, isn't it?"

Well, I'm not saying this by way of humor or derision. I'm saying it to indicate what a tremendous whirlwind that was. Now, you know the historians are slow in getting there. A long time ago Arthur Schlesinger's father, who was a greater historian, listed the great Presidents, and he brought Franklin Roosevelt in as fifth. Well, the historians are slow, but a few weeks ago they moved Franklin Roosevelt up to second. I think they're moving in the right direction, and I hope before I die—I'm only 75 years old—they will put Lyndon Johnson on the first floor, because he certainly belongs there, by every test of the Presidency.

There were two points I wanted to make if I had time. The first is that the New Deal was not the creation of Franklin Roosevelt. The New Deal was the creation of many unsung people, and it was as much the creation of the Congress as of Franklin Roosevelt. I can list many of the most important laws of the New Deal that didn't emanate from the White House at all and, in fact, had strong White House opposition. The reason it is so important for us to know this is that we need another Franklin Roosevelt, but we're not going to get one two years from now, with all due respect to the candidates, so we have to realize that there is a possibility, even without a Franklin Roosevelt, if the Congress and the American people understand the kinds of things he did.

The second point is the relevance of what Franklin Roosevelt did to today. Now, I don't mean that in the general sense of having good spirit and kindliness and being for government for the people and taking the government away from Wall Street and bringing it to Washington. That's all, you know, the run of the game. But specifically the New Deal provides an example of how we can pull ourselves back up. Our great America has been sliding downhill ever since the end of World War II, with a few exceptions. We've slid down the greasy pole. We are no longer first in influence. We are no longer first in living standards. We are no longer first in economic progress. We are no longer first in the control of inflation. We are no longer first in everything.

Now, I don't have any predatory pride in being first, but I am concerned about what's happening to the American people. And what one has to learn from the New Deal is not these academic generalities about how glorious it was, but what we do about our problems now. What do we do about the budget? What do we do about inflation? What do we do about public spending? What do we do about taking care of the unemployed?

In all these things the New Deal provides precise and exact examples of what we should be doing now. It provides an example of how to get unemployment down. We hear this canard that the New Deal didn't succeed in reducing unemployment until World War II. We've all been so brainwashed. How many of us realize that in terms of numbers and percentages, the New Deal reduced unemployment more than any administration has since? Compared with what the New Deal did on unemployment under indescribable difficulties, what has happened since has been a shocking mockery and denial of the capacities and needs of the American people and the potentials of its government if it followed the New Deal.

Those are the kinds of things I'd like to talk about if I had a little more time.

JAMES ROWE: I'm going to read four quotations. By some odd coincidence, two of them are by me.

Years ago in New York I was walking up a street and on a street corner I ran into Ken Galbraith's old buddy, Arthur Schlesinger. Now, Arthur, being an historian, never worries about the niceties of life. He started to work immediately. He grabbed me by the lapel and he said, "Do you think Franklin Roosevelt understood all the programs he put through?" I thought for a second, and I said, "I don't know, but I do know he knew how to be President." And Arthur's been using that ever since quite successfully.

That happens to be true. He did know how to be President. He never had to ask anybody what a President did. He thought, "Well, whatever I do is what a President does." And it was true.

About the New Deal I have a quotation which I have used several times—I have, in fact, used it in this room. But the audience has changed quite a bit, and the quotation's a brief one, too, I may add. It's something I wrote some time ago:

"With the possible exception of the founding fathers, there was never before and certainly has not been since the excitement, the intellectuality, the excellences, or the sense of accomplishment that existed in the New Deal, and this remembered by the hundreds, even thousands of young men and women who flocked to Washington to serve under such leaders as Franklin Roosevelt and his brain trusters."

Justice Holmes, when speaking of his Civil War comrades in a speech delivered on Memorial Day, 1884, had some words that also apply to New Dealers: "To our great good fortune, in our youths our hearts were touched with fire."

My last quotation is from a gentleman far more distinguished than I, Felix Frankfurter, professor and Justice. This is a sentence from his remarks at the graveside of Franklin D. Roosevelt, Hyde Park, Memorial Day, 1956: "Those leaders of our people abide who represent some universal element in the long adventure of man, represent qualities that kindle the heart and fortify the spirit. Franklin Roosevelt belongs to this very small band of men."

ESTHER VAN WAGONER TUFTY: The New Deal days in Washington were unbelievable, just straight unbelievable—intriguing, exciting, even explosive. Something was happening. The Depression, which had hit all of us directly or indirectly, spurred on the desire for new answers, bold answers.

I was a young reporter out of the Middle West. I'd been editor of the *Evanston News Index* in Chicago, but before that I had written for Michigan papers, and when I came to start a bureau in Washington, I mostly had Michigan papers. I also had, in the news bureau, some very bright reporters, but the brightest came from Texas—Liz Carpenter.

Franklin Roosevelt was the spearhead in that drive and search to find new, bold answers. Ideas sprang up in Washington, they sparkled over town, and every idea was looked at, examined, and weighed.

One idea belongs especially to Mr. President himself, because he launched at that time the first of its kind—the White House Press Conference. Now, this has no comparison with what you see on television today. There were only a few reporters, maybe a hundred, that could get into the oval room, and Mr. Roosevelt sat behind his desk and we stood up. We always tried to get to the front row to see what was on his desk, and some of us would even try to read the letters upside down.

The banter between the press and the President was electric and wonderful. There was an intimacy there that cannot happen today when you have two thousand press-card-carrying reporters. Besides, it couldn't happen anyway because only Roosevelt could create that kind of response and respect.

I remember one day the President had a pain across his face, and a determination. He was uncomfortable. He wanted to cross his legs, and he could not, but he looked us in the eye and he calmly took his hands and lifted one leg and put it over the other leg. The room was silent. Not a reporter in that room ever wrote a word, not even the *Chicago Tribune*.

Then there was another day. The President brought Mr. Churchill, the Prime Minister, in to meet the press. Now, you must remember at this time there was some nice, good-natured rivalry between these two great leaders: Who would be the number one man in the history books of tomorrow? Well, Mr. Roosevelt thought the occasion would not only be newsworthy—and the press were delighted—but would also put Mr. Churchill to the test by having him face a press conference the like of which he never had in London.

As we saw him that day, President Roosevelt looked tall even sitting down, but the Prime Minister was squatty seated next to him. Informality began right away when some reporter in the back of the room yelled, "We can't see him," at which he jumped up on the chair and put the victory sign up.

Well, the questions came along. I wish I could remember every one, but one I do remember. A reporter said, "How long, Mr. Churchill, is the war going to last—how long?" And he said, "Not as long if the United States is with us." So, smart man, he got his message across, too.

A lot of people thought it was politically risky to have conferences where the press could ask questions, anything they liked, to the Chief Executive, and he would answer. I remember Walter Lippmann, that august, very eminent writer, who was the only one among us who had a grasp of the great imponderables. He wanted us to have our questions planned ahead of time, but the rest of us wanted to ask questions and have the President answer right off the cuff. We were more apt to get the truth about the way the President felt.

Eleanor Roosevelt, too, contributed to keeping the President informed about what the public were worrying about and perhaps what could be done about it. Eleanor did more for women, by women, about women than perhaps any other first lady. She made a real contribution, especially to women of the press. It was very hard for women reporters to get jobs in those days, and the AP and the UPI each had to put a woman on just to cover Eleanor. She herself wrote a column, although the President said, "No, it wasn't a column; it was a diary." But she did anyway, and therefore was an active member of the Women's National Press Club.

Not only did prime ministers come to Washington, but some American queens came, too. There was a Cotton Queen from the

South. There was a Peach Queen from Georgia. This is part of the flavor of these times. Some Senator would say, "I have got the Peach Queen, and I wish that you'd go with her to take some peaches over to the President. Maybe he'll let you have a picture taken with him."

Well, once I went and took the Cherry Queen of Michigan, and the majordomo, Timmons, took the cherry pie she brought, and he said, "The President will see you." Well, these queens didn't always get in, but I guess maybe the President's day had been too routine or too troublesome, and he decided it might be fun to see a nice young girl, the Cherry Queen from Michigan.

So I went in with her, and as a lot of people know, President Roosevelt had a way of doing all the talking so that you maybe didn't get all the points across that you wanted to tell him, and this poor child had only one thing to tell him. But he asked her about the price of cherries, which she didn't know, and other questions—you know, was the crop good, and were they having trouble with caterpillars? How Franklin Roosevelt knew caterpillars were a menace to cherry trees I've never known, but he asked the question.

Well, finally, the girl said, "Mr. President"—and you knew she'd practiced this twenty-two hundred times—"I am supposed to invite you to the Cherry Festival of Michigan in Traverse City on August 4th. We hope you will come." And Mr. President answered. Of course, he didn't say yes and he didn't say no. He said, "My pretty girl, I'd sure like to come."

To close, all I'd like to say is that because of the New Deal, because of Roosevelt, Washington no longer can be described as a sleepy little southern town. It is now the international capital of the free world.

WILLIAM S. WHITE: I should point out at the outset that I'm in a rather different position from most of the people on the panel, in that I was not a participant in the New Deal. I was an observer of it. Nearly twenty-five years ago I wrote a biography of FDR entitled *Majesty and Mischief: A Mixed Tribute*. I mention this here because that title was descriptive then, as it is now, of my views toward the New Deal, of which I was an early spectator.

The "majesty" in my title was in salute to FDR's magnificent efforts to drag this nation out of the Great Depression. Certainly those days that have been described here were days when the wine of hope was really flowing in Washington. It was a marvelous time to be there.

Although people said there were a lot of crackpots in the New Deal, Lyndon Johnson put it well to me once. He said, "Well, we may have had a crackpot here and there, but we never had any pumpkin heads."

Now, to go on with the reference to my book. The "mischief" in the title referred to some domestic and foreign affairs as I saw them. Domestically I felt, as I feel now, that the memorably warmhearted Roosevelt programs for relief and recovery were marred by careless administration and by a tendency to promise too much to too many, creating great material expectations that were both unrealistic and unrealizable.

As to foreign matters, as a war correspondent in England, until I went across on D Day, I was attached to both American and British forces. Under my British cap I traveled with Prime Minister Churchill's party when he was on any mission he defined as military in nature. I recount this here because it well may be true that I fell rather too much under the influence of the Churchill view of the war, as distinguished from Mr. Roosevelt's much more sunny view.

As the whole world now knows, Churchill was deeply troubled by Mr. Roosevelt's stand on two great and fateful issues. The British under Churchill were profoundly uneasy about Mr. Roosevelt's promise that the four freedoms would prevail. They knew that these were unattainable in the real world, and that the end result of their proclamation would be a sense of disillusion and betrayal in many of those, notably the Poles, who had stood with us in the war.

Second, there was the issue of unconditional surrender, again proclaimed by Mr. Roosevelt over Churchill's objections. Churchill knew that this declaration as read by the literal German mind meant that the Allies were bent not only upon revenge but also on extirpating the German nation. The consequence of this was to madden German resistance, particularly in Normandy, to almost maniacal proportions. I saw wounded SS officers greet our medics from the ground with rifles or bayonets. Few people who were at the front in those days, I think, would doubt that the demand for unconditional surrender prolonged the war and made the task of our fighting men much more difficult than it need have been.

I recognize the reason for the proclamation. I recognize the desire to unite people here in this very strong war effort, but I did think, and I do now, it was wrong. The long and short of it is that Churchill's knowledge of history and Churchill's world view were more sophisticated in some respects than were Mr. Roosevelt's. Those who doubt this might reflect that if Churchill's strategy had prevailed, there would in all likelihood be no divided Germany today, possibly not even a Cold War, for the Russians used their lodgment in East Germany as the very basis for that Cold War insofar as it applied to Western Europe.

Finally, having said all this, in order to disclose my convictions and, if you will, my biases, I rejoice in my memories of the first New Deal, where so many people, notably Speaker Sam Rayburn and Lyndon Johnson, helped this nation with a vision and a great gallantry. I'd like to recall one more vignette of that time. I was a very young reporter with the Associated Press. That's how Lyndon Johnson and I became friends, because he was equally impoverished. He was officially the secretary to Congressman Richard Kleberg, and actually the ramrod of that office. We'd lend each other five dollars, and we would talk of a great friend.

Johnson was close to Roosevelt because Johnson had what he used to call that "can-do" spirit, and he could do almost anything and he did almost everything for Roosevelt. I mean everything legal. I don't mean anything wrong. Johnson was a tactical officer in this matter, a line officer. The academic people and the brain trusts were the strategic officers. But anybody who knows anything about war knows that while one can make very grand strategic designs, the payoff comes when you can execute those designs. Johnson did that repeatedly for Roosevelt before he'd even reached Congress.

All in all, though, I think Lyndon Johnson's view on Roosevelt was in many respects not dissimilar from mine, although he did tell me when he read my book, "I think you were too hard on him."

JOHN HOUSEMAN: There is a habit that has developed in the last few years of referring to the arts projects, and particularly the Federal Theater of the WPA, as the first example of federal subsidy to the arts in this country, but it is unfortunately not true at all. The Federal Arts Project was essentially a relief project. It just happened that among the eighteen million unemployed at the time there were a very small number of artists, and among those there were probably more actors and theater people than other kinds of artists. When the WPA was created, they were treated exactly as the other unemployed were. That is to say, they were put to work in their chosen profession, or what they said was their chosen profession. A great many people in the theater arts projects were, in fact, barely qualified as theater people. Nobody was very worried about that, because they were on the relief rolls and they might as well be working as just receiving their checks every week.

It is a great tribute to the sensitivity and the human understanding that was shown by the New Deal and in this instance by Harry Hopkins, particularly, that out of that came an extraordinary flowering of theatrical and artistic energy. It has always been said that all you need is to give an actor a trestle and four boards and enough to eat and he'll make theater for you, and that was, in fact, what happened.

The creation of the Federal Theater—the arts projects in general, the theater in particular—was opposed by the Broadway establishment, which fought it tooth and nail. They made hay on the theory that this was an attack on the earning power of the theater unions, that the checks that they were being given for work in the theater were far less than the standard rates set by the theatrical unions.

In spite of that, everybody was grateful and everybody set to work. Within one year, the leading drama critic of the country, Brooks Atkinson, said that by far the greatest energy and the greatest talent and the most brilliant results in the American theater had been achieved in the Federal Theater.

I was very fortunate. In the fall of 1936, spring of '37, in one of the finest theaters in New York, the Maximilian Theater, Orson Welles and I produced a classical play that was supposed to be just a library play, a play that had never really been performed professionally—Christopher Marlowe's *Dr. Faustus*. Because of Welles's extraordinary talent, it proved to be an artistic and popular success and ran for about four months on Broadway, an unheard-of thing.

But one night a great excitement ran through the house, because we were told that Harry Hopkins was in the house, and indeed there he was. When it was over, we rushed to greet him and to lead him backstage. I took him back to Orson Welles's dressing room, and we sat and talked for a moment, and the first thing he said was, "Are you boys having a good time?" That really was the spirit in which this relief project became one of the most creative theatrical events of recent American history, and the gratitude which we all have for that goes far beyond the fact that a good many indigent actors were kept alive, to the fact that suddenly it became conceivable that the federal government would take an interest in the arts.

In that sense, perhaps the fallacy that I spoke of earlier is disproved, because even though the Federal Theater was a relief project, I think perhaps the subsidies which today are part of our national life would otherwise have been delayed even longer than they were.

QUESTIONS FROM THE AUDIENCE

FROM THE AUDIENCE: My name is Susan Ogleby, and I'm afraid you are going to ask me how old I am, and I won't tell.

It seems obvious that you have loved being a part of such a caring, very human program, an outflowing probably without parallel in the history of the world. I was reading *A Kentucky Lawyer* the other day, and the author said, "We Christianized the federal government because we would not tithe to do the job ourselves."

I see this. I think too many so-called Christians have no twinge of conscience when they pass the sick man on the road. We seem to rationalize it now. We have paid the Good Samaritan to come along after us to take care of this rather unpleasant social obligation.

When I saw, night after night, our tent cities, our poor, our bread lines, I couldn't allow this to go on without trying to participate on a one-to-one basis. I can't tell you how many agencies, federal and state, I called to find out how I could participate with a hands-on experience. Finally, I found the soup kitchen at St. David's Hospital and I was able to collect and cook and serve. But my question is this: Has this New Deal unconsciously taken away our personal obligation to reach out on a one-to-one basis just like Christ said we must in order to be part of his kingdom?

FROM THE AUDIENCE (India Edwards): I was somewhat of a participant in the New Deal, although I was not in Washington. I did not move there until 1942. But I worked on the *Chicago Tribune* for twenty-six years, from the time I was quite a young girl. I was always a Democrat. Colonel McCormick, one of the owners and the publisher of the *Tribune*, endured having me on the paper because I came from Tennessee, and he thought that was why I was a Democrat.

I used to wear a huge FDR button during every campaign, and McCormick would look at me with disfavor, but on the whole he never said anything to me. One time his lawyer asked him, "How can you stand to have that Democrat, and a New Dealer at that, working on your paper?"

And he said, "Well, if she can stand me, I can stand her." He did stand me until I married an officer in the U.S. Department of State and moved to Washington. I had been married before and had two children, and then I married this man and moved to Washington in 1942.

In 1944 I volunteered to work for the Democratic National Committee. Some people thought it was to expiate my sin of having worked for the *Chicago Tribune* so many years. It was not. It was because I believed so fervently in the New Deal. I had the privilege of working as a volunteer during the entire 1944 convention and campaign, and the only time I ever met Franklin Roosevelt—I'd known Eleanor Roosevelt as a newspaper woman in Chicago—was when we were invited to luncheon at the White House. He was not very well, and he knew we were told not to shake hands with him. But as we went along, and one of the aides said, "This is India Edwards," he said something pleasant, and, of course, I made no effort to shake his hand. But Gladys Tillot, who was then vice chair of the Democratic National Committee and the director of the Women's Division, a very generous woman, said, "Mr. President, I do want you to know that this is the volunteer who did a very fine job for us in this campaign."

He put both hands out and he said, "Good. I'm so glad to meet you." He said, "Now you're our India. You used to be Bertie's India." They had been schoolmates at Harvard.

I consider that I am one of the most fortunate women in the world, because I had the privilege of working for a great newspaper—even though I think it had the wrong political philosophy—for twenty-six years, of working in that one campaign for Franklin Roosevelt and Harry Truman, of directing the women's activities in the Truman campaign in 1948, and then of working for Jack Kennedy and Lyndon Johnson in 1960. I worked very hard to get the nomination for Lyndon Johnson in 1960. I consider that he's one of the greatest Americans who ever lived. I think that Franklin Roosevelt and Lyndon Johnson are the two political geniuses of my time of life, and my time of life is a long time, because I am probably the oldest person in this room. I am eighty-seven years old and very glad to be here.

FROM THE AUDIENCE (Mona Jarrell): I started working with the Relief Administration when it first began, after Warner Getty set up a merit system to test people to become social workers. That was the beginning of the welfare program in Travis County.

At that time there was not enough money to pay the social workers. We were paid in kind. My check was the only check coming into my family. We got groceries every week with the twelve dollars that I began earning.

When the Civil Works Administration was inaugurated prior to the WPA, almost two thousand people were put to work overnight in Travis County. We were on the verge of a revolution here, with so many people with no money and nowhere to go and nowhere to live. They were put to work at the state hospital, they were put to work everywhere. This is where leaf raking began—WPA was called the leaf-raking project. We hear in our modern times about jobs that are not meaningful. Well, the leaf raking was only to take care of that emergency. The section I was in was called Women's and White-Collared Projects, and then it became Service Projects. We had sewing rooms. We had Housekeeping Aide Projects to put people in homes to take care of the children so the mother could work. And we had state projects in Austin, because we were the state headquarters.

But when the WPA started, then real planning began for the

kinds of projects that we had. When the Buchanan Dam project began, it was found that the area had many Indian mounds with paleontological remains in them, so the University of Texas sponsored projects to excavate. We employed through WPA, bringing in professionals (we could only employ 5 percent of these) to work with people who knew nothing about it. In this way people were given tremendous training and skills.

You can see now in your Texas Memorial Museum the results of those efforts, in the archeological exhibits. Untrained people put these together, and they are available now. All this was a tremendous boost to Travis County.

FROM THE AUDIENCE: My name is Willard Deason. I live here in Austin, Texas. My heart has really been warmed this morning by hearing so many things said about our great leader, Franklin Roosevelt.

I was a worker in the Roosevelt Army, so to speak, the New Deal Army, beginning in 1934 at the Federal Land Bank in Houston. Those of you old enough will remember that the farmers were going broke, and as they went broke and couldn't pay their loans off, the insurance companies who carried the loans were going broke, and a chain reaction was occurring. But through the leadership of Franklin Roosevelt, that trend was turned around.

I left the Federal Land Bank in 1935 at the call of my classmate, Lyndon Johnson, to go to work with him in the National Youth Administration, and that story has been told over and over. I was delighted to be a part of the Roosevelt New Deal Program.

A little personal note. My son asked me a few years ago, "Daddy, how do you really appraise Franklin Roosevelt?" I said, "Pat, when I start to heaven, if I get going in that direction, before I report to St. Peter, I plan to go by Franklin Roosevelt and ask him to validate my passport."

MRS. LYNDON B. JOHNSON: I just wanted to say that I hope we can further explore the first question from the young lady in the back, because I think it's a very important one.

I thank Roosevelt and I thank God for those programs in the New Deal that put us back on our feet and put us to work, but it did put us in peril of losing our personal responsibility for all.

Somewhere along the line, I think too many of us have begun to think that we can hand it all to the government. But the government never intended it that way. It was first aid and it was rescue, and I guess it's a philosophical question only for each one of us to answer.

But I would be sorry if that young lady back there thought that it was the beginning of deterioration in any way intended. It was our salvation at that time, upon which we all rode.

VIRGINIA DURR: Well, I certainly don't like to disagree with you, Mrs. Johnson, but I think that what the New Deal did was to rescue the people of the United States from charity. I think handing out food stamps is much better than having a soup kitchen. I think that the programs offered by the New Deal preserved the dignity of human beings, rather than making them objects of charity. I thank God the day has come when we can set up organizations that will see that people don't starve and I don't have to go out and hand them a bowl of soup.

RAPPORTEUR'S SUMMARY

ERNEST CUNEO: I will, if you please, outline to you what I think was the essence of the President's personal application and how it was delineated this morning.

When (Rexford Guy) Tugwell, (Leon) Keyserling, (Robert F.) Wagner, and the rest of that group gathered around the President, the country was absolutely flat, and they presented this thesis.

"Mr. President, there are many problems, and in the final analysis, from the Caesars to the date of these Presidents, you have but two choices, buns or bayonets." And, of course, the buns went out, but they went out in such manner as to stagger the imagination of those who had thought in terms of merely balancing the budget.

At that time, when I left to join the New Deal, (Fiorella) LaGuardia said to me, "You are going into a great adventure, Ernest, and I must tell you something. Use what ingenuity you can. Politics have driven me to many extremities, but I never sunk to disrespectability," which is in considerable part what we're facing today.

The essence of this came when the President said that he had made up his mind that Louie Dembitz Brandeis was correct that the principal assets of a country are the people who live within it and he intended to bank them. He not only banked them with Jesse Jones and a great assist from Lyndon Johnson, but the money was returned with a great profit. Now, here I must say that while these things have been in the abstract, it was a very warm and a very vital campaign.

I want to insert a word here about the contribution of Johnson as President to the realization of New Deal goals. Let me give you some figures. There were 20,000 black families in the United States making more than $15,000 when Mr. Johnson became President; there were 400,000 when he quit. There were 200,000 black families earning between $10,000 and $15,000 when Mr. Johnson took office; there were 700,000 when he quit. When I called President Johnson at the ranch to tell him this, even he didn't believe it.

Well, here I return to Mr. Roosevelt. I was present when the President of the United States sent up this message to the Congress in September of 1942:

"Gentlemen of the Congress, I have been in some doubt as to whether I should consult you at all, but I have decided to do so. Inflation is a great threat to the American people. You call it cost of living. I call it inflation. But I have here four steps: Very heavy taxation, almost confiscatory; price ceilings; price-wage ceilings; parity in farm prices. And if you do not pass this legislation by October the 1st, I shall enforce it as Commander in Chief." I suggest that the life of the New Deal was the President's absolutely fearless will to experiment and his absolute commitment to the American people.

Rostow   *Roosevelt*   *Tallboys*

II

FRANKLIN ROOSEVELT:
The Man Behind the New Deal

ELSPETH ROSTOW
JAMES ROOSEVELT
RICHARD TALLBOYS

INTRODUCTION OF SPEAKER

ELSPETH ROSTOW: The theme from the previous panel was simply that the New Deal, by necessity, federalized welfare and made the giving of assistance a public rather than a private function. We have been a country of volunteerists since the seventeenth century. In my own view, the federalization of programs did not end our concern with nor capacity to take care of our associates who need help, those in our communities who are in trouble. As I see it, the volunteeristic spirit is still alive and has been alive since the thirties, but I ask the panel to keep in mind the eloquently stated question as to whether we have lost our sense of social responsibility because we now think, or at least have thought in the past, that it was the task of government.

My first responsibility this afternoon is a delightful one. Many of us grew up with James Roosevelt. We watched him as a very young man with a full head of hair turn into a well-poised young man with less hair. We mourned this situation but appreciated that as the one item disappeared, the sense of a responsible and participating individual increased.

Mr. Roosevelt not only appeared in newsreels before us, but he had time to go to Harvard, he had time to serve in the Navy from '40 to '45, and subsequently in a career in California he has had time to serve in Congress for six terms.

He also obviously carries the sense of responsibility so characteristic of his family in other directions. He has served on boards, and continues to do so. I noted with interest that he has taught in two colleges in California and has been appointed a professor at Whittier College. He has also been a spokesman for a series of interests, including the Eleanor Roosevelt Cancer Foundation as well as many others. He now is the head of James Roosevelt and Company, business consultants, in California.

Mr. Roosevelt is going to continue one aspect of the morning by discussing his reminiscences of his father. As Franklin Roosevelt's eldest son, he not only was in a position to observe this remarkable family as a part of it, but he also has written two books on the aspects of his family that he recalls. He pays attention not just to the personality of his father but also to the Franklin Roosevelt that those of us who did not have the privilege of knowing him came to appreciate by listening to him, by watching him, some of us by voting for him, and also of course, by admiring him. It is with particular pleasure that, on behalf of the Library and The University of Texas, we welcome to this hall James Roosevelt.

REMINISCENCES OF FRANKLIN ROOSEVELT

JAMES ROOSEVELT

One of the things that I might start off by telling, which has nothing to do with my father, is a little story on Ken Galbraith. Ken and I were on a plane together from New York to London, getting in fairly early in the morning, and I was just ahead of him in the line going through the passport proceedings. The man who took my passport stamped it and looked at it and then, with a smile on his face, handed it back to me and said, "Any relation to Theodore?" I heard an explosion behind me, and Ken kind of berated the man, and said he hadn't mentioned the proper person, and then sat down and wrote a letter to the *Los Angeles Times* saying that Her Majesty should perhaps train her civilian interpreters at the Passport Bureau a little better.

Well, a distinguished colleague at Harvard heard about it or read about it and sat down and wrote Ken a letter. All the letter said was, "Of course, Ken, you know that what the passport officer really had in mind was 'Any relation to Eleanor?'"

I'm sure you will forgive me for saying that my father is not totally, in my mind, restricted to a person who had a part in the New Deal. I think of him in two separate eras. The first was prior to the time he caught polio, when he was a young man, a vigorous young man who taught me how to sail, who threw me in the water and taught me how to swim, if that was a lesson, and who did everything that one could possibly desire in an exuberant and very much alive parent.

Then, when I was about fourteen, up at Campobello Island, he contracted polio, and from then on the situation was quite different. I probably got to know him a lot better than I would have otherwise, but I also had the opportunity to see him change and grow from a rather lighthearted individual who enjoyed life to the full without feeling any too serious about it to a person forced to adjust to a confining physical condition. He suddenly found time on his hands, as probably he had never envisioned might happen. I think this gave him a stimulus to study and to work. Some of you who knew him well will remember how much time he would spend with his stamp collection. I think his stamp collection, in a way, gave him a broad vision of the world, because as he would get a stamp of particular interest, he'd delve into the country and study it and finally know more about it than even the American ambassador to that country.

As a result of this growth, I think, by 1924 his mind was moving in the direction of politics. That year he had the opportunity to make the nominating speech for Alfred E. Smith at the Democratic Convention at Madison Square Garden. In 1928 he went to Houston and nominated Alfred E. Smith again. This time Mr. Smith won the nomination, and my father decided, at the urging of my mother, to run for governor of New York. And while Mr. Smith was defeated, my father won his election by 25,000 votes. You've heard already today how he did it. People voted over and over again. So in a close election it was very conducive to victory.

I feel strongly that my father, having been elected governor, used the opportunity, during the four years prior to the 1932 campaign, to read and study and shape a strategy to do what his friends had long wanted him to do, which was to run for the Presidency.

Some of you were a part of it and will remember this group of friends. They formed what was then known as the Brain Trust, and it was made up of some most interesting, fabulous people with a really grand design. I think they built a grand design of what the government ought to do in the situation at that time, and they prepared the background material to the point that when Father was elected it was possible to move forward quickly. I completely agree with the panelist this morning who pointed out that without the Congress, the New Deal couldn't have happened. The Congress and the President working together really put a completely new stamp on the efforts of the government to revive the country.

But let me also add it was not viewed as an effort just for the masses. It was an effort to give dignity to individual human beings, to restore their confidence, to restore their hope. I've always felt that the great appeal of the fireside chats was not because of his voice, although I suppose that fit the media perfectly. It was because somehow he got across the message that he was talking to you individually, to you as a person, not to a great mass of people. As a result I think it would be fair to say that a sense of individual responsibility and opportunity was reborn, and that the American people have today an equal sense of duty toward their fellow citizens, and given half a chance they'll show it at every opportunity.

To return now to the early days of the New Deal, my real introduction to the operation was on inauguration day, fifty years ago on the 4th of March. Two days earlier, we had paid a courtesy call on President Hoover, as the incoming President is called upon to do. It was rather a tense moment, because my father had refused to participate in any of the final moves that President Hoover was proposing, and President Hoover didn't like this. He thought it was unpatriotic, and he felt it was unfair to him, because he wanted to leave his stamp on the efforts to get out of the Depression.

My father felt that this was not a wise thing to do, that he ought to come in with a clean slate, not linked in any way to the past, and he steadfastly refused to join hands with President Hoover's recommendations. So when we went over to pay this call about four o'clock in the afternoon, my father knew there were problems ahead. We were seated in the green room on the ground floor, and after about half an hour, which seemed to me a rather long time to keep an incoming President waiting, President and Mrs. Hoover came downstairs and came into the room, and there they were joined by the Secretary of the Treasury, Mr. Mills.

My father whispered to me, "Uh-oh. They're going to have one more try." And sure enough they had one more try, and again the proposal was turned down. So after about ten minutes, Father saw that the President was getting a little nervous, and so he said, "Mr. President, I guess it's time we should take our leave. I hope you'll understand that my heavy braces make it impossible for me to move very quickly, and so if you don't mind, I'll just stay seated until you and Mrs. Hoover have retired, and then I'll take myself and my family down below."

President Hoover drew himself up and in rather a clearcut voice said, "Mr. Roosevelt, when you become President you'll find out that nobody leaves the room before the President of the United States," Two days later, when we were driving to the

Capitol for the inauguration, there were quite a few people on the sidewalk and along the route, and I noticed that my father was taking off his hat and bowing and answering the people who were greeting him on the side. Mr. Hoover was sitting there absolutely stonefaced and not saying a word to anybody. As we went by the new Archives Building, which was about one-third completed, I suddenly heard my father say, "Mr. President, isn't that beautiful steel in that new building?" And Mr. Hoover went, "Huh." And that was the total conversation from the White House to the Capitol that day.

I might also explain to you how I happen to have one Republican brother. After the inauguration was over, we had a family dinner that night, the first meal in the White House. We were finished about eight-thirty, and my brother Johnny, my youngest brother, said to my father, "There's a dance up at the Mayflower Hotel, and I'd like to go up." Father said, "Fine, fine. Go ahead, but remember the gates of the White House are locked at one o'clock."

Well, in those days we didn't have the security that they have nowadays. The gates were locked with a chain and a padlock, and there was one guard in the guardhouse next door. Father said, "You better get in, because he'll be asleep by ten minutes past one, and he won't let you in."

So you know what happened. Johnny got back at three o'clock in the morning and rattled the gate until finally the sleepy guard came out and said, "What do you want, young fellow?" And Johnny said, "Well, I'd like to go to bed." And the guard said to him, "Well, young fellow, this is not a hotel. This is the White House."

Johnny had driven his old jalopy down from Harvard, and as the guard looked around him, he said, "And by the way, do you own that heap of junk?" Johnny said, "Oh, yeah. It took me all the way down from Boston to here. It's not junk. It runs fine." And the guard said, "Any young fellow who drives that kind of a jalopy does not sleep in the White House," and he wouldn't open the gate.

So Johnny went back to the Mayflower, came down about half past eight the next morning, and he said, "I know you're a Democrat, Father, but if a Democratic President can't somehow get his son in at any hour of the night to sleep in the White House, from here on in I'm a Republican." And he stayed that way all the rest of his life. I never quite understood it.

To reminisce a little bit further, I think one of the reasons my father was successful as a political figure was because he had such interesting and diverse people around him. His first Secretary of the Treasury was a man called Will Woodin. Mr. Woodin was chairman or president of the American Car and Foundry Company, hardly a small company in those days. He was quite a big wheel, but he was very slight, very small. And if you remember, the biggest job immediately at hand was to close the banks and then reopen them.

The Cabinet met one evening to devise a plan to close the banks and reopen them with as little panic as possible. They were still in session about three o'clock in the morning, and my father, knowing that they were close to exhaustion but had not reached a conclusion, suddenly stopped everything and said, "I thought we might be in rather a long session, so I asked Will Woodin if he wouldn't entertain us. Let's take a fifteen-minute break." Will Woodin reached behind his chair, drew out his violin, and for fifteen minutes we listened to the most beautiful music you ever heard, played by the Secretary of the Treasury.

And then there were people like Harold Ickes (Secretary of the Interior). My father started early infiltrating the Republican Party. He pulled a Republican out of Chicago, because he knew if things had to be put to a vote, he'd better have a Republican on his side. But what I always loved about Mr. Ickes was that he was willing always to be the lightning rod. Father once said to me, "You know, Harold is the greatest sport in the world. If I want to try something out, to send up a trial balloon, I tell Harold, 'You've got a new idea. I think a lot of it.' " Then Mr. Ickes would try it out, and, of course, if it went off, Father immediately adopted the idea as his, but if it fell down, then it was Harold Ickes's idea all the way through. I suppose that's what my wife calls dirty politics, but there's a practical side of things that you have to think of.

Life wasn't always serious, always difficult. I know that even in the early days, whenever Congress was about to adjourn, Father would assemble what he used to call the "Cufflinks Club." The Cufflinks Club was made up of old friends and some new friends, people like Marvin McIntyre, who had been with him since 1920,

Steve Early, and others. They would gather around and play poker, and the rule was that the poker game went on until the Speaker of the House and the President of the Senate called up and said, "Mr. President, we have no more business. We're ready to adjourn. Do you have any final message for us?" And, of course, the President never did.

The rule of the poker game was that when that call came in, there'd be one more round and only one more round. On one of these occasions Father whispered to me, "I'm in trouble." I looked around, and Henry Morgenthau, who was a part of the poker game, had collected the biggest pile of chips you ever saw in front of him, and nobody else had hardly anything. Father said, "We're going to play a little game on him." He said, "Now, you call up and tell the Speaker that when he gives the message, you are going to reply loudly enough so we can hear it at the poker table, 'Oh, you'll be in session another hour? Oh, Mr. Speaker, that's too bad.' Then hang up quickly and come back, and we'll go like mad for one more hour, and then, of course, we'll finish with the round because Congress will have adjourned."

Well, in that hour Henry Morgenthau was cleaned out, absolutely cleaned out. But unhappily he read the next morning in the paper that Congress had adjourned an hour earlier. And those of you who remember Henry will not be surprised that he came over and said, "I cannot work for a crooked President. I hereby resign." And for the second or third time we convinced him to withdraw his resignation.

I remember other things, some of which were a little bit personal. In 1941, I was working for General William Donovan as a member of the Marine Corps, and the intelligence agency that later became the CIA was formed. I didn't want to join that very much, because that wasn't my particular kind of work in the Marine Corps. So I asked if I could be excused. About a week later, Father called me in, and he said, "I'm going to send you and Major Thomas on a very important secret mission." I said, "What's that?" He said, "I'm going to send you to the Middle East. I'm going to send you with some gifts for each of the potentates in the Middle East, but with a special message to them. My intelligence tells me that they are flirting with the idea of joining Hitler and Mussolini." And he said, "That would not be good at this point at all. It would hamper our efforts greatly. I

Above: President Roosevelt, accompanied by his wife Eleanor and eldest son James, go to the White House after the first inaugural ceremonies on March 4, 1933.

Opposite page: (top) FDR visits the CCC Camp at Big Meadows in Shenandoah Valley, Virginia, on August 12, 1933. Seated at the table are (l-r) General Dudley F. Malone; Presidential Assistant Louis M. Howe; Secretary of the Interior Harold Ickes; CCC Director Robert Fechner; FDR; Secretary of Agriculture Henry A. Wallace; and Presidential Adviser Rexford G. Tugwell.

(bottom) President Roosevelt signs the historic Social Security Act, August 14, 1935. Standing are (l-r) Rep. Sam B. Hill; Rep. Robert L. Doughton; Sen. Alben Barkley; Sen. Robert F. Wagner, Sr.; Rep. John Dingell, Sr.; Secretary of Labor Frances Perkins; Sen. Pat Harrison; and Rep. David Lewis.

Franklin D. Roosevelt Library Collection

Wide World Photos

51

want you to convince them that at some point we probably will be getting into the war and they better stay out of it because certainly they don't want to get in on the losing side, and if we get in, we're going to win."

So I paused for a minute, and I said, "Now, wait a minute. Don't we have a Neutrality Act? Suppose King Faruk drinks a little bit too much one night and talks about the message that you've just given me to give to him and it's published back home in the newspapers. What happens to me?" "Oh," he said "you've violated the law and you'll be indicted." And I said, "Well, then what?" He said, "Well I'll just repudiate you. That's all I'll do."

I might add we went on the mission, and it's all detailed in Washington in the Marine Corps Museum, and the Arab potentates did not get in on the Hitler side.

At the same time, I think that we were all very aware of the fact that there were tremendous pressures. We witnessed on the domestic scene the rather difficult business of the effort to pack the Supreme Court, as it was sometimes known. We did what we could, but somehow in our bones we didn't think we were going to win. I'd like to share with you the fact that while the main intention, from a public point of view, was to pack the Supreme Court to make it change its mind about the constitutionality of New Deal affairs, the effort also reflected my father's belief that the judicial system needed a considerable reformation. Attorney General Clark had devised a reformation which appealed to him and he felt the fight was worth making and went to it. Whether he later changed his mind, I really don't know, but the rest of us, I think, felt right away that it was an ill-fated gesture.

There was one other happening which I think historians, because of the recent findings of a committee, are going to pay more attention to, and that was the putting of the Japanese-Americans into concentration camps. Many of you will remember that and will also remember that it was, in the opinion of most people, clearly unconstitutional. The fact that it went on for the duration of the war, that the Japanese-Americans were just swept out of the West Coast, taken into these concentration camps, and deprived in many ways of what they prized in their American citizenship, seems terribly unfair, ill thought out, and unfortunate. And so it was.

But if you had lived on the West Coast at that time and had

seen, as I saw, on the faces of so many people utter terror any time they saw anybody that looked like a Japanese, after the submarine fired its shell into a refinery along the coast of California, you would understand that the danger to the Japanese-Americans themselves from emotionally stirred-up Americans was undoubtedly a part of the reason that the edict was finally issued.

I think as time went on, even though he didn't have enough time to think about it and change it, that was one of the things that my father would certainly have liked to change. I stress this because above all I like to have people think of my father as a human being. He was not a god. He could make errors, and did make errors in many, many ways, but he also had a vision—a vision that probably from the time he got polio grew in nature and in stature.

This was shown best in many small ways. Down in Warm Springs, Georgia, Edsel Ford had built him a Ford touring car. The top could go down, and he could operate it totally with his hands—he didn't have to use his legs in any way. This enabled him to go out on the back roads, and the Secret Service car was too wide to follow him, so he'd lose them pretty soon. There he was all by himself, or with a companion, driving along, and he'd come upon a farmer on the side of the road, and he'd stop and talk to him and they'd get to be friends. And he'd ask him about his crops, and he'd ask him about his cattle, ask him about the water situation, and about the fertility of the land. You could really see that he felt the land must be cultivated, the land must be preserved—he was a conservationist. And through this kind of contact, not only did he develop the opportunity to talk to the ordinary person without the trappings of the Presidency alongside him, but he also used this perspective to develop the total program that he had in mind.

My most memorable reminiscences are the four inaugurations. It meant a great deal that he trusted me to be with him on these and other occasions. I stood up with him at all four of them. I was with him at the declaration of war at the Capitol following the 7th of December, 1941, and we were very close in a lot of ways.

So I was a little astonished when I was out in the South Pacific in about December of '44 and got a letter from him which simply said, "I'll see you before inauguration day in January." I wrote back to him and said, "I can't leave the Pacific. We're training to go to Okinawa, and there's not really any way that I could leave my command." In about five days, I got a personal message that the Commander in Chief wanted me in Washington on the 20th of January. And the admiral on whose staff I was serving said, "I think you'd better obey orders."

So I went back and saw him for the last time in that January of 1945. I was, of course, greatly distressed because, to me, he had lost a tremendous amount of his physical health and capability. His doctors insisted on telling me that there was nothing wrong with him, that a few days at Warm Springs would revive him entirely, but I knew that something was definitely wrong.

As we finished the inaugural ceremony on the south lawn of the White House, he asked me to come in with him for a moment. He said, "I can't go through the reception. I'm too tired." Then he told me that he had left some things for me; if anything happened to him during his term of office, I was to go in, open his safe, and carry out certain things that conveyed his wishes concerning his funeral arrangements and other matters.

I said to him, "I don't think you need to be that pessimistic," but he said, "Well, I'll feel on the safe side."

On that same occasion he brought up two other matters of significance. Many of you will remember Missy (Marguerite) LeHand. Missy LeHand was my father's right arm, in a way. She'd been with him from way back in the 1920s, and she had lived as part of the family, and then she had a stroke. When she had the stroke, Father called in Mr. O'Conner, his law partner of former years, and said to him, "I want you to put something in the will to take care of Missy in case she has difficulty getting over her stroke." When Father told me the gift was still in the will, I said, "But Father, she died quite a while ago now." He said, "Yes, she died all right, but, you know, I changed my will with Dr. O'Connor once. If I go back and change it again, believe me, I would rather do anything in the world than have to fight Doc O'Connor, he's such a difficult man." He told me this so that I could explain to people later why the will was never changed.

So the gift to Miss LeHand stayed in his will, and historians afterwards have written about it and tried to impugn something that wasn't pleasant for a lot of people to read. But I assure you it was there because he had a sense of loyalty, which he demonstrated to his family and to many of his friends, as far as I know, practically all the time.

And then finally, I said to him, "You know, I don't know when I'll be back. We're going to finish Okinawa in short order, and then we're going to make a landing on Japan, and that's going to be a bloody affair. We're going to really have a tough time with that one."

He looked out the window for a moment, and then he turned around and said to me, "You'll never make that landing on Japan." And you know, I must have been an utter fool. It didn't imply anything at all to me, except that we might have some new surprise method or some new landing schemes, or something of this kind. So I never paid any attention to it.

But a few months later it came to my mind that maybe that was his way of telling me that the atom bomb was on its way. Ever since then I've wondered whether the bomb would have been dropped exactly in the same way if my father had been alive. Certainly I don't mean it as a criticism of President Truman and the way he handled it. Everybody, certainly the President, had a terrific responsibility, and it must have been a burden that was almost impossible to bear. He made the decision based upon the evidence that the military gave to him and told him about the possibility of a misfire, the possibility that dropping the bomb would not be safe.

But I've always felt in my own mind that my father would have found a way to give it a little more exposure, to show the Japanese the terror of it, the effectiveness of it, so that it would not have been dropped on such a large civilian population. That's only my opinion. I don't have anything to back it up with, my friends of history and academic distinction in the audience, but I'm sure of one thing, because I had a part in talking to Mr. Einstein and various other people: Father's use of the atom bomb was something that was on his mind constantly from the time that it was born. It's probably the best kept secret in the history of the country, and it was certainly a tremendous surprise to the enemy.

Now, finally, let me bring you to the end by telling you that when my father died I was out in the South Pacific. The Navy was wonderful to me and made every effort to get me back in time for the funeral, but I failed because of headwinds. Unfortunately, this meant that I was unable to remove the things from the safe in the White House, but because my father had communicated much of the information verbally to my mother, most of the arrangements had been in accordance with his wishes.

When I arrived in New York, I made arrangements to meet my mother coming down on the presidential train to take her back to Washington to pack up and leave the White House. Then I felt the need of some exercise, so I walked up Park Avenue. It was quite a lovely sunny day. When I started down the other side—it was about five-fifteen in the afternoon—a taxicab pulled up to the curb, and the driver jumped out. He looked at me and said, "Are you who I think you are?" And I said, "I don't know who you think I am." But then I said, "Yes, I'm President Roosevelt's son." And he started to cry, and he told me about how his family had been saved and how it might have been broken up and how much he owed to my father's Administration.

Then as he was about ready to get back in the cab, the fare in the back seat, who obviously had come up from Wall Street, leaned out of the cab and yelled at the driver, "Get back in here, young fellow. I'm not paying you to cry over that fellow who should have been dead years ago." There was a horrible silence, and then, quick as a flash, the driver opened the door, reached inside, took this middle-aged man by the scruff of the neck, dumped him on the sidewalk and drove off.

I was at least two blocks away by that time. But it made clear to me that anybody who does anything in the world—and I think that President Johnson would have felt the same pressures—knows that there will be people who love you, there will be people who admire you, but there also will be people who disagree with you, even to the point of hatred.

The hope, then, that I would have for all our leaders is that they have the courage to be hated as well as loved, and that at the same time they know and have the sureness that they are on the right track, the sureness they need to carry out and experiment and to come up with unusual answers.

I think of my father as a human statesman, but above all I think of him as a beloved father.

INTRODUCTION OF SPECIAL GUEST

ELSPETH ROSTOW: Mr. Roosevelt, there is not a parent in the room who would not wish to have at some time in the future a child say of him or of her what you have said of your father.

Let me now tell you that we have, as the LBJ Library has from time to time, a surprise for you. The surprise is a mystery guest. I will introduce him, but I will not reveal the reason for his being here. He will reveal it.

Our mystery guest is Richard Tallboys, born in Tasmania, educated both in his home country and in England. He served as Lieutenant Commander in the Royal Australian Navy, and after a career suitably decorated, he became Her Majesty's Consul General in Houston, a post he has occupied since 1980.

Mr. Tallboys.

RICHARD TALLBOYS: I was very, very young indeed at the time of the event which this gathering celebrates here today, and throughout the Second World War I was a mere schoolboy in England. During much of that period I was at my home in the direct path of the air raids on London. But although only a schoolchild, I was left in no doubt as to the debt that Britain owed to the United States and to the personal support that our country was receiving from President Roosevelt.

At school we were, as a matter of course, taught the words of the "Star-Spangled Banner," which I might add in the two-and-a-half years I've been in Texas has proved to be a very useful thing to have learned. Those words and the sound of the Roosevelt radio voice, his image in photograph and cartoon, are as much a part of the memories of my boyhood as are the experiences of the bombing raids and the doodlebugs, the latter word being the invention of an ingenious American serviceman.

I am of a generation that was just too young to participate in the struggle of 1939 to 1945, but I was old enough to realize to whom we owe the opportunity to live free from tyranny and to bring up our own children in a free democracy.

As one of that generation of Englishmen, it gives me a special pleasure, therefore, to be here as Her Majesty's Consul General to read to you a personal message to this symposium from Her Majesty Queen Elizabeth, the Queen Mother:

"The name Franklin Delano Roosevelt is associated above all others in the minds of the British with the support that the United States gave to the United Kingdom in the dark days before and during the Second World War, but quite apart from remembering Mr. Roosevelt's role as a world statesman, I, with countless others, have also many pleasant personal recollections of President and Mrs. Roosevelt.

"Through the invitation the President extended to us, the King and I visited the United States in June 1939 and were perhaps able at a critical time to play some part in strengthening the relationship between our two peoples. I still have many warm memories of that visit, including the day at the President's home, Hyde Park, where we experienced our first American picnic complete with very delicious frankfurters.

"That visit to the United States was both successful and enjoyable because it was based on friendship between us, both as individuals and as nations. The natural kindness and hospitality of Americans will always be for me a happy memory.

"We were sorry that the President could not in his turn accompany Mrs. Roosevelt to Britain in October 1942, but I am pleased to learn that Mrs. Hobby, a wartime colonel who did accompany her and whom the King and I met in London, is still playing an active part in the affairs of Texas.

"At this gathering in Austin to mark the fiftieth anniversary of Mr. Roosevelt's inauguration as President, there will undoubtedly be many whom my husband and I met either on our 1939 visit to Washington or elsewhere during the Roosevelt years at the White House. I am sorry that I cannot be with you to share recollections of his life and work and to reflect with you upon the remarkable changes that have taken place in our world since the 4th of March 1933.

"Such recollections would remind us not only of the role that Mr. Roosevelt played as an international statesman, but also of his humanity and his friendship. Present and future generations will remember with gratitude his vital part in ensuring the freedom that the people of Britain and of the United States continue to enjoy."

Signed Elizabeth R., Queen Mother

ELSPETH ROSTOW: Thank you, Consulate General. On behalf of the Library and the University, I accept with pleasure this important and historical message from the Queen Mother. It will continue to occupy an honored place in this library.

Rostow

Leuchtenburg  *Louchheim*  *Freidel*

McLaughlin  *Mitchell*  *Nash*

Cater

III

THE POST-NEW DEAL ERA

ELSPETH ROSTOW
WILLIAM E. LEUCHTENBURG
KATIE LOUCHHEIM
FRANK B. FREIDEL
CHARLES C. MCLAUGHLIN
CLARENCE M. MITCHELL, JR.
GEORGE H. NASH
DOUGLASS CATER

INTRODUCTION OF SPEAKER

ELSPETH ROSTOW: William Leuchtenburg, born in New York, was educated in that state at Cornell and at Columbia, and after a brief career elsewhere, including one year in Cambridge, Massachusetts, he went back to New York and has remained at Columbia, rising through departmental chairmanship to become the DeWitt Clinton Professor in 1971. At present, he also holds the William Rand Kenan Professorship at the University of North Carolina at Chapel Hill.

But Bill Leuchtenburg is much more than that. I tried to count the number of books that he's written, and I stopped somewhere around twenty-two. The one that most of us remember, perhaps the best, is the reason that his presence here is so appropriate. It's *Franklin D. Roosevelt and the New Deal,* a volume which appeared in 1963 and which won both the Bancroft Prize and the Parkman Prize.

He has written extensively on the American twentieth century, and I don't know any historian who can top him in terms of his perception of this period and also in terms of his capacity to describe complex issues with clarity, with pungency, with wit, and insofar as any human being can tell, with accuracy.

THE SHADOW OF FDR: PRESIDENTS FROM TRUMAN TO REAGAN

WILLIAM E. LEUCHTENBURG

This is a short drama in three acts.

Act One. On April 12, 1945, Vice President Harry Truman was presiding in the United States Senate over a long, dull debate on a water treaty. When the debate ended shortly before sunset, he made his way over to the office of Sam Rayburn to join his friends for their usual afternoon round of bourbon and branch water. No sooner had his drink been poured than the Vice President was told to call the White House. The President's Press Secretary wanted him to come down right away, quickly and quietly.

Truman put down the phone, raced through an underground tunnel in the Capitol, and sped to the White House. When he got there, Mrs. Roosevelt came up to him, put her arm on his shoulder, and said softly, "Harry, the President is dead."

Franklin D. Roosevelt had died that afternoon in Warm Springs, Georgia. After a moment of shock, Truman recovered himself to ask Mrs. Roosevelt, "Is there anything I can do for you?" She replied, "Is there anything we can do for you, for you are the one in trouble now."

That was an odd remark to make to someone who had just ascended to the highest office in the land, but Truman grasped immediately that he was indeed in trouble, for so totally had Roosevelt embodied everyone's notion of who the President was that it seemed incomprehensible that anyone else could be President of the United States.

Many Americans could not remember when there had been anyone in the White House but Roosevelt, and they'd assumed without thinking about it that he'd be there forever. In the 1944 campaign, according to one story, a man said to a loyal Democrat who had just become father of a baby boy, "Maybe he'll grow up to be President." "Why?" the father replied. "What's the matter with Roosevelt?"

Often Truman did not receive even the minimal respect due to a man who held the same office that Roosevelt had adorned. On his first morning in office, he phoned Jesse Jones to report that the President had appointed a St. Louis man to be Federal Loan Administrator. "Did he make the appointment before he died?" Jones asked. "No," Truman replied, "he made it just now."

Like Andrew Johnson, to whom he was often compared, Truman faced all the difficulties that his predecessor bequeathed him, especially all the vexatious problems of conversion from a wartime to a peacetime economy, and he bore the blame for everything that went wrong, blame that Roosevelt, by his timely death, escaped.

During the 1946 campaign, Truman's stock fell so low that the Democratic National Chairman, Bob Hannigan, told him to stay out of sight, and the Party turned to recordings of Roosevelt's voice instead. In one radio commercial, a discussion of the meat shortage, a voice announced, "Here's what President Roosevelt had to say about it," although the shortage had developed after Roosevelt was in his grave. The radio audience then heard Roosevelt discoursing on the leading problem of the Truman Presidency.

The Republican National Chairman denounced this ploy as one of the cheapest and most grisly stratagems in the history of American politics. It was bad enough for Truman to be humiliated by having to take second place to a dead man. Worse still, the Party, running for the first time without Roosevelt in the White House, went down to defeat in the midterm elections, and Truman was blamed for lacking FDR's magic touch.

It was seriously suggested that Truman resign from office, like a British Prime Minister who has lost a vote of confidence, an idea that a number of people in the Roosevelt circle rushed to endorse. The notion originated with Senator Fulbright. Ever thereafter Truman referred to him as Senator Halfbright.

In 1948, Truman made an altogether unexpected comeback by following a strategy outlined by Jim Rowe of basing his campaign on an appeal to memories of Franklin Roosevelt and the New Deal. But, even after his remarkable upset triumph in 1948, Truman could not get out from under Roosevelt's shadow.

Analysts credited the outcome not to Truman but to Roosevelt, for forging the winning coalition. All Truman had done, they said, was to scrape by on the basis of the combination Roosevelt had put together. One of Winston Churchill's American correspondents held a similar view. The victory, Churchill was told, was a consequence of FDR's New Deal party system. The author of the letter—Harry Truman.

The aftermath was even more troubling. Truman had all along viewed his role since 1945 as being that of a caretaker President, carrying out Roosevelt's fourth term, but now he'd been elected in his own right, and he thought everything would be different. It was not to be.

Critics regarded the Fair Deal as little more than warmed-over New Deal, and one observer characterized Truman's tenure after 1948 as Roosevelt's fifth term. When the attacks on Truman for failing to measure up to Roosevelt continued into his new term, Truman came to take a more questioning look at the Roosevelt heritage, in one respect in particular. Nearly three years before his term was scheduled to expire, Truman decided not to run for reelection because he disapproved of his predecessor's example in breaking the two-term tradition. In a memorandum that he wrote for posterity in April 1950, Truman stated,

> There's allure in power. It can get into a man's blood, just as gambling and lust for money have been known to do. This is a republic, the greatest in the history of the world. I want this country to continue as a republic. Cincinnatus and Washington pointed the way. When we forget the examples of such men as Washington, Jefferson, and Andrew Jackson, all of whom could have had continuation in office, then we will start down the road to dictatorship and ruin. I know I could be elected again and continue to break the old precedent as it was broken by FDR. It should not be done.

To Truman, it could not help but seem manifestly unfair that he was still being perceived as Roosevelt's stand-in, but he had reason to think that there were other ways that history might judge him than merely as FDR's successor. He was, after all, associated with developments that were only remotely related to the Roosevelt legacy, or not related at all: the Marshall Plan, the Berlin Airlift, the dismissal of General MacArthur, the emergence of civil rights as a national issue.

To a degree, this was recognized, but Truman never managed

to walk out from under the giant shadow cast by FDR. A contemporary journalist summed up Truman's difficulty: "His deepest misfortune was to replace a Roosevelt rather than a Harding, and to face each day the exacting challenge of comparison with his predecessor."

Years later, Truman made a one-sentence comment that encapsulated his experience: "Heroes know when to die." He was commenting on the greatness of Abraham Lincoln, but in a way that left his interviewer with a question. Was he making an analogy between Lincoln's death and that of Franklin Roosevelt? It became clear that this was exactly what he was doing when Truman began to talk about Lincoln's successor, Andrew Johnson, the man with whom he clearly identified.

"It took about eighty years for the truth about Andrew Johnson to come out, but it finally did, and now people know what kind of President he was," Truman said. "Johnson had gotten into such trouble," he went on, "for one reason. He tried to carry out his predecessor's policy."

The interviewer pressed on with another question: "What would have happened if Lincoln had lived?" This embraced a different but similar inquiry: "What would have happened if Roosevelt had lived?"

Truman's response provided the answer to both questions, the explicit one and the implicit one. "If Lincoln had lived, he would have had the same experience," Truman stated, "but like I said, heroes know when to die."

Act Two. Ten days after Franklin Roosevelt was inaugurated in March 1933, a prominent financier wrote to him, "I just stopped off at Providence to see my oldest daughter at the Sacred Heart Convent. The mother superior of the convent, a real saintly woman, said the nuns were praying for you, and then made a remarkable statement for a religious woman to make, that since your inauguration peace seemed to come on earth. In fact, it seemed like another resurrection." The financier who sent Roosevelt this report was Joseph P. Kennedy.

Five years later, when a former Secretary of State met with Joe Kennedy, he found a very different attitude. Henry Stimson noted in his diary, "Speaking of the effect of the New Deal upon himself, Kennedy said that a few years ago he thought he'd made money enough to provide for his children. He now saw it likely to be all gone and he lay awake nights over it."

These two episodes indicate the boundaries of the attitudes toward Roosevelt that John Kennedy absorbed as a young man, and it may help to explain his failure to share the enthusiasm of others of his generation for FDR. The signals Jack Kennedy received became even more confusing after December 1937, when Roosevelt appointed his father Ambassador to Great Britain.

On the one hand, Jack, who was then a junior at Harvard, understood that Roosevelt had bestowed a singular honor on an Irish Catholic by naming him his country's envoy to the Court of St. James. On the other hand, the President became increasingly disturbed at reports that his Ambassador was saying that the Nazis could not be defeated, that the Jews were running America, and that Roosevelt would go down to defeat in 1940. The rumors of hostility toward Roosevelt within the Kennedy family gained added credence when, as a delegate to the 1940 Democratic Convention, Joseph P. Kennedy, Jr., who was being groomed for a political career, voted to deny Roosevelt nomination for a third term. He was the only Massachusetts delegate to refuse to change his ballot to make FDR's nomination unanimous.

As the time of the 1940 election drew near, it was clear that Joe Kennedy's days were numbered. On the day the Ambassador returned to America, the President was lunching with the young Texas Congressman Lyndon Johnson when the phone rang.

"Ah, Joe, old friend, it's good to hear your voice," the President said. "Please come over to the White House tonight for a little family dinner. I am dying to talk to you. You've been doing a wonderful job." Then he hung up the phone, looked at Johnson, and drew his forefinger across his throat like a razor.

Joe Kennedy sat out the war a bitter man, hoping for some high post from Roosevelt, but never hearing from him. Worse was still to come. During the war, Joe Kennedy, Jr., the apple of his father's eye, was killed, and Joe Kennedy never forgave Roosevelt for it. In April 1945 the nation was plunged into grief by the death of FDR, but Joe Kennedy wrote his daughter, "There is no doubt that it was a great thing for the country."

A year and a half later, Jack Kennedy was elected to the House of Representatives for the first time; but as Congressman, no doubt because of the ambiguous signals he'd received from his father at a critical stage, he showed a conspicuous lack of inclination to identify himself as a Roosevelt liberal. True, he often voted with New Deal Democrats, but not always and with little ardor. Furthermore, he more than once traced the country's difficulties in foreign affairs to a sick Roosevelt at Yalta.

As a consequence, he aroused the suspicion of a number of liberals, most particularly of Eleanor Roosevelt. When Kennedy sought the Democratic vice-presidential nomination in 1956, he ill-advisedly tried to line up the former first lady on his side, for she was known as the keeper of the flame. Instead, Mrs. Roosevelt embarrassed him in a public place by asking him why he had not spoken out against Senator Joe McCarthy.

Kennedy had made himself particularly vulnerable on this question by writing a book with the title *Profiles in Courage*. This opened him not only to the gibe that he should have shown less profile and more courage, but to Mrs. Roosevelt's celebrated comment, "I would hesitate to place the difficult decisions that the next President will have to make with someone who understands what courage is and admires it, but has not quite the independence to have it."

Kennedy, for his part, demonstrated little interest in assuaging the doubts of the Roosevelt liberals, but in 1960 a change came. When Kennedy sought the Democratic presidential nomination that year, the pollster Lou Harris told him that it was essential for him to identify with FDR if he hoped to win the critical state of West Virginia, where pictures of Roosevelt could be found in almost every miner's home.

Kennedy took this advice. He offered himself for the first time as a New Deal liberal and imported Franklin D. Roosevelt, Jr., to campaign for him. In one speech, FDR, Jr., said, "My daddy and Jack Kennedy's daddy were just like that" (gestures closeness), a notion that astonished those with long memories but attracted the electorate. In addition, at Joe Kennedy's suggestion, thousands of letters with FDR, Jr.'s signature were shipped north and then mailed to West Virginia voters with the proper postmark, Hyde Park, New York. On the basis of such appeals, Kennedy was victorious in West Virginia, and that put him well on his way to winning the presidential nomination.

As President, Kennedy adopted policies that drew upon the New Deal and showed an abiding interest in the style and performance of Franklin Roosevelt. It was almost as though Kennedy, for whom Roosevelt had literally been a household word, was just discovering him. Still, for all of his interest in

Roosevelt, for all of his efforts to cultivate the Roosevelt family, for all of his indebtedness to particular ideas of the earlier period, Kennedy did not think that the Roosevelt legacy was really pertinent to his own times.

On one occasion, holding up a memo from a White House aide, he said to a caller, "Look at that, will you? Seven single-spaced pages, and what a lot of blankety-blank. I dearly love this man. He has a fine mind and some fine ideas, but in this case," he paused and said with a trace of a smile, "he is proposing that I conduct myself as Franklin Roosevelt did in 1933, but this fellow can't get through his head that, first, I'm not FDR and this is 1963, not 1933."

If Roosevelt never cast as large a shadow over Kennedy as over Truman, or as he would over Lyndon Johnson, Kennedy nonetheless never escaped the presence of Franklin Roosevelt, no more in death than in life. No sooner had Kennedy died than historians and publicists felt compelled to assign him a place in history, and once more comparison to Roosevelt seemed inevitable. Some regretted the fact that Kennedy's premature death denied him the chance to roll up the achievements of a Franklin Roosevelt. "It was," wrote Arthur Schlesinger, Jr., the sympathetic biographer of both men, "as if Roosevelt had been killed at the end of 1935." Yet Roosevelt had accomplished much by 1935, and other writers emphasized how thin Kennedy's record was.

But while this historic assessment was going on, something more important was happening. Kennedy was becoming part not of history but of myth, a myth that much of the public embraced and that historians could not altogether escape. As Theodore White has written, "More than any other President since Lincoln, John F. Kennedy has become myth. Unlike Franklin Roosevelt, Kennedy was cut off at the promise, not after the performance, and so it was left to television and his widow Jacqueline to frame the man as legend. Like the youth on Keats's Grecian urn, he would prevail oblivious to time."

Had Kennedy lived, he could not have escaped comparison to Roosevelt, and he may well have been judged never to have measured up to him, but by becoming part of myth rather than history, Kennedy was at last outside the shadow cast by FDR, a shadow that had been first cast when he was Joe Kennedy's young son. This is an irony that John Kennedy, who never lost his sense of ironic detachment from the world, would have been the first to appreciate.

Act Three. Final act. A short time after Harry Truman left Sam Rayburn's office on the afternoon of April 12, 1945, a young Congressman showed up. He'd first come to Congress in the spring of 1937 in a special election. Only twenty-nine years old, he had run as an outright supporter of FDR's controversial court-packing plan.

The press had said that everyone was against the plan. The special election would be the first test of how the American people really felt. When the young outsider was victorious, the country hailed his triumph as a vote of confidence for Roosevelt. The President himself was so pleased that when he came to port from a fishing vacation, he made a point of greeting the young man.

As they rode together, Roosevelt advised him on what to do when he reached Washington, and gave him Tommy Corcoran's phone number. It was in such fashion, as Franklin Roosevelt's prótegé, that the new member from Texas, Lyndon Johnson, came to Congress.

Washington quickly reached the conclusion, as Mrs. Durr said this morning, that Johnson was FDR's pet Congressman. Roosevelt once was heard to remark, "That's the kind of man I could have been if I hadn't had a Harvard education."

When in Sam Rayburn's office Johnson learned the news of Roosevelt's death, he was grief stricken. As William S. White reported in a memorable account, Johnson's eyes filled with tears and he said, "He was like a daddy to me always. He was the one person I ever knew anywhere who was never afraid."

When, in November 1963, Johnson succeeded to the Presidency, he declared openly that Franklin Roosevelt was his model. If as President he was in Roosevelt's shadow, he gave every indication of purposefully stepping into the shade. He relied upon counselors from New Deal days, like Jim Rowe, and drew upon experiments of the FDR era. The National Youth Administration (NYA) served as the basis for the Job Corps.

When he was the President's chief assistant, Bill Moyers once told me, "Johnson's relation to FDR was like that of Plato to Socrates. He was Roosevelt's pupil. Roosevelt may not have known this, but Johnson was always studying him. The influence of Roosevelt on Johnson," Moyers said, "is like the mark a prehistoric river leaves in a cavern. If you go to someplace like the Lore Caverns, you may not see the old river, but you sense its presence everywhere."

Johnson, in short, gave almost every indication that he wanted nothing more than to be a Roosevelt follower, to serve his memory loyally, and to perpetuate his ideas. In fact, President Johnson wanted a great deal more than that. He had gargantuan ambitions. He would not be content to go down in the history books merely as a successful President in the Roosevelt tradition. He wanted instead to be, in his words, "the greatest of them all, the whole bunch of them."

And to be the greatest President in history, he would need not merely to match Roosevelt's performance, but to exceed it. On election night, 1964, when Johnson watched returns at the Driskill Hotel in Austin, reporters expected him to be jubilant over his rapidly building landslide victory over Goldwater. They were startled to find him peevish instead.

He had no doubt that he was beating Goldwater. He was cranky because he was still not sure that his percentage was greater than FDR's in 1936, for Johnson was not running against Goldwater. He was running against Roosevelt.

When I spoke to President Johnson at the White House in the fall of 1965, he made clear to me exactly how he measured himself against his predecessor. Johnson said of Roosevelt, "He did get things done. There was regulation of business, but that was unimportant. Social Security and the Wagner Act were all that really amounted to much, and none of it compares to my Education Act."

Johnson was unwilling merely to remain in Roosevelt's shadow, not only because of vaulting ambitions, but because in one crucial aspect Johnson thought of FDR not as a model but as a bad example. You remember that he'd come to Congress in 1937 on the court-packing issue, and that was the most important single memory of Johnson's earlier years. He had seen a President win an overwhelming victory at the polls and then have an expectation explode only a few months later when the court-packing bill went down to defeat. The New Deal would never be the same.

Johnson, too, had just won an overwhelming victory. Over

lunch, in 1964, after the election, he told reporters that he meant to avoid Roosevelt's error. One of those present that day, Tom Wicker, writes, "Lyndon Johnson said he would not throw away the fruits of his great victory for some unattainable goal as Roosevelt had done in trying to pack the Supreme Court, but," Wicker adds, "he did."

Johnson's difficulties came, of course, in foreign affairs, where at least as much as in domestic policy Franklin Roosevelt served as his model. Johnson was certain that in acting as he did in Vietnam he was doing only what Roosevelt would have done. In the 1960s Johnson looked at the situation in Vietnam through spectacles ground in the 1930s. Not only did he analogize the challenge in Southeast Asia to that posed by Hitler at Munich, but he even proposed to establish a Tennessee Valley Authority in the Mekong Basin.

But by 1968 President Johnson had come to realize that, like Roosevelt, he had made a critical policy choice that carried a very high price, far more costly for him than for FDR.

To some it seemed that President Johnson's decision not to run for another term meant that at last the country was no longer in Roosevelt's shadow, that he'd encountered trouble because he tried to apply FDR's ideas in a time when they were no longer germane. Thus, the historian Eric Goldman, who served on Johnson's White House staff, has written: "America had been rampaging between the 1930s and the 1960s. The alterations were so swift, so deep, that the country was changing right out from under President Lyndon Johnson. Johnson, acting upon the kind of policy that would merely codify and expand the 1930s, was about as contemporary," Goldman writes, "as padded shoulders, a night at the radio, and Clark Gable."

Implicit in such analyses is the assumption that the FDR legacy is no longer usable, that President Johnson's last year spelled the end of the Roosevelt tradition. But this assumption is highly questionable, for to a remarkable degree Roosevelt continues to cast a shadow, even if that shadow appears to be waning.

When Jimmy Carter launched his presidential campaign in 1976, he calculatedly chose Warm Springs, Georgia, and when he addressed the country on the energy crisis, he deliberately picked the format of the fireside chat.

Inevitably, Roosevelt has had greater meaning for Democrats

than for Republicans. It has been said that the shortest book in the world is the book of Irish oat cuisine. A book on the impact of FDR on Gerald Ford's Presidency would be even shorter.

Dwight Eisenhower is frequently characterized as the man who preserved the New Deal and made it permanent. In fact, Eisenhower did not much care for Roosevelt and deplored much of the New Deal.

Richard Nixon, though, surprisingly, frequently found occasion to cite Roosevelt, and a former Attorney General of the United States recently told me that he was often struck by how Nixon modeled himself on FDR, not in his program, but in his presidential style.

Most extraordinary has been the performance of Ronald Reagan. At the 1980 Republican National Convention, Reagan quoted from FDR so liberally that the *New York Times* entitled its editorial on the convention "Franklin Delano Reagan." But that is far from being the whole story, for on more than one occasion Reagan has insisted that the New Deal derived from Mussolini, despite all of the evidence to the contrary. Whatever talents President Reagan may have, an extensive knowledge of history is not one of them.

Yet at other times, Reagan has spoken with the greatest warmth about the New Deal, and he has an almost compulsive need to return to Roosevelt. Frequently, Reagan attempts to reconcile his inconsistency by saying that he admires the Franklin Roosevelt who ran for President in 1932 on a platform of balancing the budget; that he, Reagan, has never changed, only the Democrats have changed. But that claim overlooks the fact that Reagan voted for Roosevelt not just in 1932 but in 1936, 1940, and 1944.

Reagan, in fact, once described himself as having been a hemophilic liberal, and he has never fully gotten over his hero worship of Franklin Roosevelt. Just last year, I heard the President say at lunch at the White House that Roosevelt was the first President he had ever seen, at a parade in Des Moines in 1936. Reagan said, "What a wave of affection and enthusiasm swept through that crowd, drawing from us a reservoir of affection that we did not know we had in those hard times. It was from Franklin Roosevelt, an American giant," the President declared, "that I first got a sense of the majesty of the office I now hold."

In 1983, as we commemorate a half century of the New Deal, it seems clear that no one will any longer live in FDR's shadow, as each in his fashion, Harry Truman, John Kennedy, and Lyndon Johnson did, but it will be a considerable time still before the shadow vanishes forever.

PANEL PRESENTATIONS

ELSPETH ROSTOW: We now turn to the panel, and I turn to a pleasurable task of introducing the chairman of the panel. Katie Louchheim would appear to be strictly a politician were I to tell you that she was appointed by President Kennedy as Deputy Assistant Secretary of State, the first woman to hold so high a post in that Department. She would also sound wholly politician were I to add that President Johnson appointed her to the Executive Board of UNESCO with the personal rank of Ambassador. All this is true.

She would also sound like a public figure were I to enumerate the boards that she has adorned and the public services she has performed, but the record would be incomplete because, in my eyes, basically, Katie Louchheim is a poet. She has two volumes to her credit. One won a prize. The other should have won more prizes. She's also written an autobiographical account, *By the Political Sea*, which describes the political scene in this country through the perceptions of someone who is both an activist and a poet.

She is now not only partly in New York but also partly in Chatham on Cape Cod. Nevertheless, she keeps a vigilant eye on this nation's affairs, as she has done for a few years. A New Yorker by impulse, she has now returned to her hometown, and we are particularly glad that she has also come to this town.

KATIE LOUCHHEIM, CHAIR: I particularly want to say to this audience that I have very few credentials. I think the reason I am here is because of my late husband, Walter Louchheim, who became a member of the New Deal. I would have not known about the politics, I would have not known about the history of this era had it not been for him.

I recall the circumstances under which it all began. My husband, who had given up Wall Street, was working on his philosophical thesis on the Aristotelian theories of logic and time when the *New York Times* arrived in the building. I saw a headline about the Securities and Exchange Commission and ran upstairs and did everything to distract him, and finally said to him, "Look, this is the Securities and Exchange Commission. You have always been on the floor, and the affluence there did not attract you, nor did you think it smelled very good. You thought it was quite crooked. Go down there and enroll." He did and he became the thirteenth employee. So that's why I'm here.

I got interested in writing about the New Deal when some young man said to me he had never heard of Richard Whitney. Some of you will remember that Whitney was the art thief of the Stock Exchange and was eventually sent to Sing-Sing. I decided that the future generation had better be reminded of this, and I therefore have taped those New Dealers who were actually participants in the endeavors of the time and who enjoyed themselves in the fashion they sometimes find difficult to express. There will be a book on this subject, and I hope all of you will read it. It will be out in the fall. (*Making of the New Deal: The Insiders Speak*, Harvard University Press, October 1983). I hope that through it the spirit of the New Deal will live, for I feel that the enthusiasm, the camaraderie can only be described by those of us who participated in it.

FRANK FREIDEL: We have been charged to talk about the effects of the New Deal to the present. I think the real bridge between this morning's comments and our charge of this afternoon is in the question that came up and was debated at the end of the morning session: Are we today our brothers' and sisters' keepers or not? I think here we face a dilemma, a problem to which there is no really good answer.

I have been bothered recently by the feeling that we have the safety nets in place thanks to the New Deal, that the greatest contribution of the New Deal made to later years was Social Security, regardless of what flaws there may be in it, but that these safety nets have affected many people's sense of personal responsibility for the poor. A common feeling seems to be, "Well, I am paying my taxes for these programs, and therefore if these people are having to sleep in automobiles and are in bread lines it is their own fault. The government is doing something for them or should be doing something for them, and therefore we do not really have to dig into our own pockets."

Then, on the other hand, there is the serious question of what would it be like if we didn't have these safety nets, if we depended entirely upon tithing or upon charity, with people of all faiths, all colors feeling that they had to take direct responsibility themselves? And that made me think back to the early New Deal years, which I do remember. I am much too young to be reminiscing, but I can remember what it was like—it pains me even to say so—to be living in a household in which the father who had always had a good job and a considerable amount of income, over two or three years was gradually using up every resource the family had to the point that one could come home one day and find that there was no food in the house, there was no prospect of food, there was no prospect of a job, and the family was going to have to go on relief. The humiliation of this had been implanted in everyone in the 1920s. Obviously this was felt to be a personal failure, not simply a national failure at the time of depression.

I feel, therefore, that the form of relief the New Deal provided was positive in several respects. A person had the opportunity to exchange skills for food and money. The jobs programs did a great deal not only to preserve skills but also to preserve self-respect. And if there is one thing that Franklin D. Roosevelt was insistent upon from the very beginning, it was his own feeling that people should not—for moral reasons, for their own good, for the nation's good—be getting something for nothing.

What would the alternative have been? I'm afraid the alternative wasn't really very good. I don't want to bring out horror stories on what pittances people were able to receive from the Red Cross and other organizations. The fact is that not many people had enough money to give, that the borrowing power of individuals for these purposes was not like the borrowing power of the federal government. Not even state borrowing power would suffice. And while there were those individuals, as there are today, who opened their hearts and their coffers and gave extremely generously, the sad fact is that this was not true of everyone.

I was deeply upset several years ago when I read William Harbaugh's wonderful biography of John Davis, the Democratic candidate for President in 1924. Here was a man who felt that it would be absolutely wrong for the federal government to give money for relief, that it should be done by private charity. Davis did indeed give. What Harbaugh found he had given was $1,000 of an income of nearly $100,000. So for many reasons I feel that it was absolutely vital to this nation to have the safety nets in place.

Franklin D. Roosevelt said again and again that having federal aid or state aid or local aid was not enough, that every citizen still had a responsibility, for these two things went together. I can only say that this still holds true today.

CHARLES MCLAUGHLIN: What I thought I would tell you about is some extrapolation from what might be called enforced or involuntary research on one side of FDR's life. I am here today partly because of some voluntarism on the part of FDR himself. The innovations that he encouraged in the treatment of polio at Warm Springs and the beginning of the Polio Foundation, before he became President, were things that bore fruit for me in the summer of 1955 when, with three thousand other people in the city of Boston, I succumbed—and so did my wife—to polio. And it was the innovations of FDR and the Foundation that literally saved the lives of one-half or three-quarters of the people who were in the hospital with us. We saw iron lungs. We saw rocking beds. We tried out Canadian canes. We got therapy, continuous therapy for the rest of our lives, if needed. And all of this happened because FDR not only fought the noble fight, the personal fight, against polio, but because he was far-seeing enough to realize that major innovations should take place in the treatment of the disease. So in this sense I am very lucky to be here, and I can very personally thank FDR for that legacy.

During my period of enforced confinement and research, strangely enough, besides reading *The Magic Mountain,* I read *Roosevelt at Warm Springs,* and in that I began to identify and try to analyze. As a historian, I am in the business of trying to empathize with people's activities in the past and the problems they have faced, and so I began to think about what polio might have done to FDR. People say, "Well, it turned him from a supercilious young whippersnapper into a great-hearted politician." I'm not altogether sure that was true. I would suspect that what polio did for Roosevelt was to intensify qualities that were already well implanted in his psyche and character. But I did gain some insight as I pondered this question further in my enforced retirement.

One thing that I discovered in talking with Harry Murray, a Harvard psychologist, was that Roosevelt had a somewhat schizoid attitude toward polio. Harry Murray was a young intern at Bellevue Hospital when Roosevelt was brought in from

Campobello, and so he watched his recuperation in the hospital and went to see him every day. He said that normally when interns go in to see patients, what the patients want to know is: "How am I doing, Doc? When am I going to get out of here?" And, to be sure, that's exactly the kind of questions that were asked in the hospital where I was for a year. But Harry Murray went on to say what FDR discussed with great élan were his yachting prints, and he would display his collection every time Murray came in, or they would talk about contemporary events or literature, but they never talked about polio. I realized that he was in a way schooling himself to go beyond, to transcend the disease. Yesterday I watched for the first time the inauguration of 1932, which was an incredible thing to see. To see FDR come down stiff-legged—unless you had a practiced eye, you wouldn't have realized anything was wrong with him—and then to see the energy that went into that address was a remarkable experience for me.

There was a line, a famous one, in the inaugural—"We have nothing to fear but fear itself"—which I could see had an analogue in his own physical experience. The one thing that actually paralyzes anybody who has an imbalance or muscular weakness is fear. The courage that FDR obviously had throughout his life had to be intensified just to ignore the fact that gravity pulls quite hard and that occasionally a fall is inevitable.

So these are some basic things that I feel he learned, but then there were deeper, shall we say, more intimate things that he must have learned in a completely cold and unrelenting, unforgiving school of physical disability. The first one was the need for bold, persistent experimentation. A person in that kind of situation is always thinking of stratagems, of ways of working through his best remaining abilities to get out of bed, to get upstairs, to get across a hall. You learn to experiment and to improvise at every turn—you do not want to restrict your mobility by refusing the next challenge.

Another thing one discovers, particularly in the earlier phases of this disease, is that it is an optimistic disease. It's not like multiple sclerosis, where you have a degenerative, continuous downhill slide. It is an unexpectedly optimistic disease. I can remember sitting on my bed, having been cranked up to receive people coming in to see me. I said, "You know, I used to be able to lift my arm over my head," and there it was. And I suddenly realized that in the early stages of the disease, as the swelling goes down nerves suddenly come back that you never expected to be able to use again. There is also a slow buildup of stamina and vitality, and because you don't expend quite so much physical energy as other people, you have a kind of endurance that goes on into the night and that other people can only envy.

Then another thing I learned and am sure Roosevelt must have learned is that when you are in a dependent situation, you identify with people who are in many other ways in dependent or exploited situations. You also learn, when lying flat on your back, that simple things—like needing your big toe moved or wanting the window shade pulled down—become very urgent, very compelling, and that the people you deal with should not be overwhelmed with your needs. You feed them to these people one at a time because we are a democratic society and you don't want to come on like Louis Quatorze.

The last thing that I discovered, to my annoyance at first, was that all of a sudden you are visible, that you are suddenly a superstar wherever you go. You are always noticed. You are always remembered. If I were a politician and had a good memory for names, this would be a grand thing. You come to know not only the cop who directs the traffic where you cross in your wheelchair, but also all the back ways in the Lyndon Baines Johnson Library and where the trash goes out because that's where you go out. In a way, all this could be seen as training for politics. Obviously I'm not President of the United States, so it hasn't done me that much good, but FDR was able to move in that direction.

The other side of this superstar element is that you crave invisibility occasionally. I discovered the only way to get invisibility and to have other people react normally was to drive a car. All of a sudden I was back with the human race, to be honked at and shouted at out of windows. It also provided a fantastic mobility—I could move about by myself and relate to other people. And so hearing the tale about how that car got fitted up for FDR by Edsel Ford, I understood completely. When I learned to drive all over again, I loved doing it, and I have since then done all the driving in our family, including two trips across the country.

One final story. I met another polio patient in California who had been to Hyde Park recently and had been quite annoyed because there were no facilities for the handicapped. He said a caretaker there had said, "Oh, well, there is this elevator over in the corner. I think the last person to use it was FDR; it's a hand elevator." He said, "Good, I will go use it." So my friend was the next person in line at that elevator.

CLARENCE MITCHELL: You know, there are always people who are trying to rewrite the Ten Commandments and put the Lord's Prayer on the head of a pin and things like that, and they miss the big point of what the great goals that we have been seeking in this world are all about. I think that in this country we have forgotten—and perhaps some people never knew—what it is we came together to achieve.

We came together as a nation to give life and dignity to the idea of freedom, equality, and justice. Throughout our long history, from the colonial period almost down to the present, we had never had the guts, g-u-t-s, to face up to the obligation that ideal imposed until a tall Texan from this area came to the United States as the President, bit the bullet, and declared that he was going to see to it that in this country, as a matter of law passed by the Congress of the United States, we could get rid of the idea that blackness is a sign of inferiority and that people should be consigned to a state of unequal treatment simply because of the color of their skins.

My first vote was cast for President Roosevelt when I was twenty-one and just finishing college, without a job. I got a job because of the Blue Eagle, and, needless to say, I'm grateful to Mr. Roosevelt for that. Thereafter I served as an assistant director of the state National Youth Administration program. I'm grateful to Mr. Roosevelt for that.

On June 25, 1941, Mr. Roosevelt issued that great executive order setting up the Fair Employment Practice Committee (FEPC), which put our nation on record as saying that we believed in equality in the job area. And, of course, I am eternally grateful to Mr. Truman because Mr. Truman was the person to whom we appealed to end the disgrace of segregation in the armed services of the United States. And I'm pleased to say it was part of my mission to try to accomplish that result. I am very grateful to Mr. Truman for what he did in those areas. So what I am about to say about Mr. Johnson is not in derogation of those gentlemen, but only to say as a historical fact that all of them were willing to accept the doctrine that as a matter of law, it was proper to have something called "separate but equal based on race." None of them had the troops, the courage, or the perspicacity to stand up and say, "It is a disgrace to have a situation in the United States of America where the government of the United States, where the governments of the states, where the governments of the cities countenance segregation and discrimination based on race." If you look at every single program that we had in this country before Mr. Johnson took his heroic stand against discrimination per se, you will see each one of them was flawed by a treatment of separation based on race. We had it in the National Youth Administration. We had it in the great housing programs, where the government of the United States went on record sanctioning segregation in housing made possible by federal funds.

At the time when we were attacking Adolf Hitler because of his racism, because he was saying that there is such a thing as superiority based on color of skin, we were saying to the black men who wanted to be in the United States Navy, "You can only be in if you want to be stewards and messboys," and nobody wanted to do anything about it. We were saying to a black man who was willing to take up arms and fight in the Battle of the Bulge when the Germans broke through, "Well, we will grudgingly give you an opportunity to be part of a segregated armed services." And while I am grateful to people like Mrs. Anna Rosenberg and others who worked with us when we were trying to end segregation in the armed services, it was Mr. Truman who went farther than anyone else in trying to eradicate that stain from our nation. But thereafter we went back into the old way of saying, "Yes, black children are entitled to go to public schools, but we don't think they ought to go to school with white people"; went back to the old way of saying, "Yes, we'll have a plan where we will put people in hotels and restaurants because they are travelers, but we've got to have those blacks in separate hotels and restaurants"; or, "Yes, we've got to have a situation where people have an opportunity to be educated, but they've got to be in separate colleges and universities."

Above all, we took that position in the matter of jobs. Mr. Roosevelt had started us off with the fair employment practice concept, but it was an awful task keeping that alive. I was the person who tried to do it in Washington through various executive orders. It was not until Lyndon Johnson sounded the trumpet, acting in the tradition of great people like Abraham Lincoln, that we were able to say in the Congress of the United States, "We are going to pass legislation which will assure that there will be equal treatment in the job area, that when the government of the United States spends money it will be on a nondiscriminatory basis and a nonsegregated basis, and that will assure that we will eradicate discrimination from the voting places of our country." No other President had dared to take such a bold stand as that. And I say to you Mr. Johnson does not live in the shadow of any of his predecessors; he stands like a mountain of importance in our national history, and I for one shall forever be grateful that he was given to us by God to lead this nation into a status in which I was not ashamed to stand up as a United States delegate at the United Nations and declare that this is the greatest of experiments in democracy, because I knew what Lyndon Johnson had tried to do, and I knew the extent to which he succeeded because of his sheer determination. I never thought of him and do not now think of him as standing in anybody's shadow, not even the shadow of Abraham Lincoln.

Now, I am particularly grateful that we have here in this audience people who have assured us that the Roosevelt legacy is not dead, and that the Lyndon Johnson concepts of how to make that legacy even greater, how to influence it and make it more attractive with his own ideas, shall never die.

I look out at that front row, for example, and see Jim Roosevelt. Now, Jim was a member of the Congress of the United States when we were trying to write into the law the equal employment opportunity concept which, under President Roosevelt's order, was called the Fair Employment Practice Committee. And to show you how intelligence plus a little skill and maybe a sense of humor can change things, we had been calling that the FEPC. This was a fight word in Washington. Any time you said FEPC, that was raising the red flag, recreating the Civil War, having your daughter marry a black man, and all kinds of things. So one day Jim said to me, "Clarence, I think if we change this from

FEPC to EEOC, maybe we would diffuse some of the opposition." We did that, and I would say to the representative of Her Majesty's government that I love that line, "Confound their knavish tricks," and I say to you that we were able to confound their knavish tricks. When they got up with their speeches ready to attack FEPC, we said, "What are you talking about? We are for EEOC," and they were demolished. But we could not have done that if we had not had a man who, as somebody said, thought of President Roosevelt as his daddy. He was willing to bite the bullet. He was willing to lay his prestige on the line when a whole lot of people were ready to run for cover.

And if you don't believe it was important, look at the papers of day before yesterday and today, because there you will see a steel settlement up in the state of Pennsylvania with millions of dollars going to black workers who were the victims of discrimination. They are getting those millions because of the Equal Employment Opportunity Commission which started out as the FEPC under Jim's father, which Jim himself picked up as a torch and carried on, making it EEOC, and which President Johnson got legislated despite filibusters and all other kinds of obstructions.

And there also sits on that front row my beloved friend, Lynda Johnson Robb. Look at the paper today, where you see that in the state of Virginia, a settlement has been achieved on an EEOC case, again involving millions of dollars going to state employees. This again is the fruition of what started as the Fair Employment Practice Committee and came through as the Equal Employment Opportunity Commission, making it possible, according to the press, to get that settlement, which does justice to millions of blacks. Much money is going into their pockets that they wouldn't have gotten otherwise because her good husband, the Governor of the State of Virginia, adopted a policy in the same courageous manner that President Johnson adopted policies and said that the state of Virginia will not oppose justice when it is being sued to give fair treatment to people who are the employees of this state. Now, that kind of courage, it seems to me, is the kind of courage that we don't seem to have a high regard for.

I look at what the historians have written and read the books of different people. I have spent the greater part of my life in Washington, and I see a very different picture from what they see. They seem to see civil rights as a kind of minuscule operation and

I see it as the vindication of the dream of the founders of this country. Without it we wouldn't be any better than Hitler's Germany.

If we in the United States had continued the kinds of policies that were sort of glossed over and tolerated by everybody before Mr. Johnson, I could not in good conscience have sat before you today and said that I saw any difference between the government of the United States and the government of South Africa. I am pleased to say that because of my experience over the years with these able people—allies from the labor movement, people from the churches, the heart of America following the leadership of a great President implementing the dreams that started out under Mr. Roosevelt—I was able to stand up when Idi Amin came into the United Nations and to say before the parliament of the world, "So far as I am concerned, I do not tolerate racism whether it comes from a black mouth or a white mouth. I am against racism, and I am against what Idi Amin stands for." I could not have said that if I had not known the kind of progress we were able to achieve because of the dedication and leadership of people like President Johnson.

So I say to you I think we have to stop trying to analyze, capsulize, microscope-ize, and do all other kinds of things to show the seamy side of our leaders in this country. All of them have done things that are worthwhile. All of them have been great and wonderful people. I think it's probably true that much of the criticism that is leveled against President Johnson because of his handling of the Vietnam War is not because of what he did with the Vietnam War; it's because of what he did for blacks in this country. That's just a kind of a screen behind which people hide. They are basically racist and they don't have the nerve to come out and say, "Well, we're against Johnson because he believed in the equality of blacks and he gave them an opportunity to get into the mainstream of America." They therefore jump on him about Vietnam and some other things. I think it's a disgrace that in our nation there are people who try to downgrade the President for some picayune thing when they ought to be saying that the President stood up at a time when it was crucial to the survival of this nation, when we were having riots in the streets, when people were being beaten simply because they were riding in the nonblack section of the bus.

It seems to me that we have come to an era in this country when we have to face the fact that there is just too much carping, too much effort to downgrade and chip away at the greatness of the people who have led us along the way. And I hope that what will come out of this observation is a realization that we have been the luckiest nation in the world because these great people have led us. Each in his own way stands distinct: President Roosevelt, President Truman, and President Johnson. I think that we ought to be mighty thankful for that, and so far as I am concerned I never, never will speak apologetically about what was accomplished.

I want to end with an example of how progress has been made. We had a big riot down in Mississippi on the Gulf one day because the blacks went out to bathe in the Gulf of Mexico. Can you imagine anybody trying to segregate the waters of the Gulf of Mexico? Well, anyway, that's what they did. And the question was this: What kind of a legal handle can the federal government use to get into this? Well, the legal handle came about in this way: There had been a big storm on the Gulf that had washed away a lot of the sand during the Roosevelt Administration, and it was fixed with funds from the WPA. But there was a provision in that agreement that the beach would forever be open to all people in the public, even though it was in front of all those beautiful hotels. So through the legal reasoning of the WPA, which was incorporated in an agreement with the State of Mississippi, the federal arm was able to attack the matter of discrimination on the waters of the Gulf of Mexico.

I am pleased to have been invited down here, and I am eternally grateful for having had an opportunity to know and understand the contributions of these people that we have been talking about. There will never be anyone who can replace the memory of Mrs. Roosevelt and the great things that she did. There will never be anyone who can replace the things that President Roosevelt and Mr. Truman did. But above all, I must confess that dearest to my heart I cherish the memory of Lyndon Johnson because he has kept alive in this country the ideals that we were supposed to be trying to achieve when the nation was founded.

GEORGE NASH: In one of the panels yesterday, Professor Leuchtenburg said that the function of a commentator is to be mischievous, and I suppose such is the function of a Hoover biographer at an FDR and New Deal symposium.

Actually, it is not my purpose today to bring you greetings from the old order, nor is it my purpose to pronounce anathemas on what succeeded the Presidency of Herbert Hoover. But I do come to you from a perspective rather different from that of most of the commentators thus far. As I look at the impact of the New Deal since the 1930s, I see certain elements that strike me as leading us to a somewhat more ambiguous assessment. What I say will perhaps seem to have a Hooverian overtone, although it is not my purpose here to discuss Herbert Hoover.

In 1936, my father was in his early twenties. In that year, my grandfather died, the family business closed, and my father's family confronted the grim plague of the thirties—unemployment. The next winter, my father obtained a job with the WPA. He was assigned to work with a crew digging a ditch and laying a water pipeline in his hometown. This was in Massachusetts. As it happened, it was a bitterly cold winter and with no protective blanket of snow on the ground, the zone of frost bit deep. To dig the ditch, it was necessary to penetrate down through three feet of frozen earth using wedges, sledge hammers, and pick axes. It was agonizingly slow work. To dig a section of a ditch just five feet deep in all, one-and-a-half feet wide and eight feet long, it took two men two entire days. It was work, of course, and the pay, though meager, was welcome.

But my father and his fellow workers wondered why it was necessary to dig that ditch at the worst possible time, in the dead of winter. If the WPA had simply waited until spring, the frozen earth would have thawed and the pipeline could have been laid rapidly with far more efficiency and far less cost.

Such instances of misallocation of resources of so-called makework projects evoked popular ambivalence. On the one hand, the projects gave the unemployed, including my father, something to do and precious pay besides—short-term benefits. On the other hand, the projects frequently conveyed the impression that the work at hand was hardly worth doing or worth doing well. A subtle disjunction between effort and reward developed. A certain attitude of cynicism took root—long-term lessons. It was said that the initials WPA stood for "We Putter Around."

This experience of my father illustrates in microcosm some of the principal legacies of the New Deal. In the short term, the WPA and various other New Deal agencies, which we have heard so warmly remembered this morning, provided emergency assistance to millions of Americans in real distress: food, money, mortgage relief, and more. Millions benefited. In doing so, the New Deal, as George Will wrote last year, "irrevocably altered the relationship between the government and its citizens."

"We hold this truth to be self evident," declared the Democratic Party platform of 1936, "that government in a modern civilization has certain inescapable obligations to its citizens, among which is aid to those overtaken by disaster." It is a principle that is now embedded in our national consensus. Today, few dispute that one function of government is to provide, in contemporary terms, a safety net for the truly needy.

But in providing humanitarian aid and in establishing the federal government as the prime purveyor of that aid, the New Deal had a consequence that has proved increasingly problematic. In the perspective of half a century, it seems clear that the New Deal's fundamental achievement was not the restoration of prosperity but the founding, however embryonically, of the welfare state. And the fundamental premise of the welfare state is that the redistribution of wealth is the principal purpose of government. But where, one must ask, does the wealth come from in the first place? Will there always be wealth to divide? What, after all, is the source of our prosperity? What is the engine of job creation and productivity? In what ways can we assist people in need without creating a permanent culture of dependency? How can we establish a safety net without succumbing to the demoralizing proposition that the government owes everyone a living, not just a subsistence but a living? These are troubling questions and ones which, as we all know, increasingly impinge on our public discourse.

I would like to give you one example, and I will not choose it from the United States, partly because I don't want to get into contemporary controversy and partly because it illustrates a point I want to make, namely that the crisis of the welfare state is one that transcends the United States and is not simply due to the programs, good or ill, of the current Administration. It is a problem being faced by governments throughout the industrial world.

While preparing for this panel, I came across a remarkable article on the efforts being made now by West European governments to control the welfare state which in principle has been accepted. No one disputes the principle. But the application is now coming under some scrutiny. And I came across some interesting data about Holland, which is one of the most advanced of the modern welfare states.

The unemployed in Holland receive benefits for two-and-a-half years, much longer than in the United States. Unemployed workers receive vacation pay. Holland's social security benefit program absorbs 35 percent of all government spending. But what I find most remarkable is that under the disability insurance program currently operating in Holland, incapacitated workers are allowed to spend the rest of their working lives receiving 80 percent of their previous pay, adjusted annually for inflation.

This is a program undoubtedly noble in conception, but what has panned? It seems that it is very difficult to lay off a worker in Holland. It requires approval of government—regional councils, involving a great deal of red tape. Companies circumvent this procedure in the following fashion: They approach the worker and suggest that he declare himself disabled. The common excuse given is low back pain. The workers don't mind going on the disability program because the benefits are very generous, so they stay at home for a year on 80 percent of their pay under the government's sick-pay program. At the end of the year, it is common for the disability plan's medical service to declare the worker permanently disabled. What has happened in practice is that 750,000 workers in Holland have now declared themselves disabled. That's 15 percent of the entire work force. What has happened, I'm afraid, is that a program noble in conception has somehow become flawed in practice, and it illustrates the point I made earlier.

Irving Kristol has defined a neoconservative as "a liberal who has been mugged by reality." Someone has defined a neoliberal as "a liberal who has been mugged by reality but refuses to press charges."

I'm reminded in closing of the early twentieth-century journalist Ambrose Bierce's definition of a conservative and a liberal. "A conservative," he said, "is a statesman enamored of present evils, as opposed to the liberal, who would replace them with others."

Today, fifty years after the Great Depression, it seems to me that we confront the disturbing and ironic reality that the welfare state and the principles upon which it rests have themselves become an impediment to prosperity and social well-being. Improvising boldly, responding to human misery, the New Deal gave Americans hope and it gave them immediate relief if not a permanent cure. As Mrs. Johnson put it this morning, it gave America first aid. This was its fundamental achievement. But in the long run, it bequeathed also a philosophy of government that, taken alone, cannot suffice. Self-evident truths can become half-truths unless balanced by other truths gone out of fashion.

QUESTIONS FROM THE AUDIENCE

FROM THE AUDIENCE: I would like to ask Dr. Nash to address the issue of justice rather than compassion. I just saw the farm workers in South Texas, who make an average of $2,900 a year working very hard while the growers make millions. Rather than giving people welfare, what about giving people the chance to earn a decent living for their work?

GEORGE NASH: I think the fundamental conservative response to that is that the best welfare program, the most equitable program, is a prospering economy. Some statistics suggest that over the 1940s and '50s, as the economy increasingly prospered, the number of people dependent on government decreased. So I think the first answer would be that.

The second answer would be to point to the terrible difficulties of trying to substitute what I shall call political judgment for marketplace judgment when it comes to trying to improve people's lives. I think there is a tendency among those who would look affirmatively on the New Deal as applicable to today to feel that a political allocation of resources would be accepted as an equitable allocation of resources. My reading of the situation is rather different. It does seem to me that the more the welfare state as a political redistributive apparatus impinges on the total society, the less equitable society is perceived to be, because everyone begins to say, "Well, he got his way because government gave him a favor," you see. In other words, we think, "Well, the government is all of us; it's democratic, therefore we will be satisfied." But it strikes me that dissatisfaction increases proportionately as we are conditioned to turn in a total fashion to government.

So I think it's very difficult for a conservative to say that the plight of those to whom you referred would be improved by a reliance on a greater redistribution of income, a greater involvement of government in the marketplace.

FROM THE AUDIENCE: I really don't want to get embroiled in everything that we're hearing in the news, but how was the Social Security Act envisioned at its time of inception, and how long will the latest compromise put off our problems? I really get the impression that it's just putting things off.

WILBUR COHEN: When Franklin D. Roosevelt inaugurated the Social Security Act of 1935, he thought of it just as a beginning. He knew that he couldn't get the whole thing through and he knew that we did not have the competence to administer it, so he established it only for old age benefits with the hope that future generations would build on it. In 1939 he recommended the first great addition to it, life insurance, which immediately increased all the life insurance in the United States 100 percent. It doubled the extension of life insurance in 1939.

During the war, he intended to add health insurance to the program, but that did not get completed. President Truman, as I reported earlier, said that he would add the health insurance as President Roosevelt had intended. And so President Truman in 1945 gave his famous health insurance message. Later the disability and Medicare portions were added as a logical part of the total retirement package.

So answering your question, the original purpose was to begin with old age benefits and then to add a complete package of old age, survivors', disability and health protection. That was certainly within the President's original intention.

Your second question was how long will the latest compromise—the one recently passed by the House Ways and Means Committee that will come up in Congress next week and pass the House of Representatives—last? It will, on the basis of present analysis, carry the system until the year 2035. I don't think you need to worry too much about next week or the week after that, but if you want to worry about the year 2025 or 2035, yes, there may be problems in the future. But I would also add if there are problems, they also exist for the entire economy, including all the private pension plans in the United States as well as the welfare that private corporations enjoy by virtue of their tax exemptions. That is as much a form of a welfare state as Social Security is. They enjoy it equally as much and, in some respects, quite extravagantly as compared to beneficiaries of the Social Security Act. But I don't think you need to worry until at least 2025 or 2035 that the present compromise will not keep the system sound.

FROM THE AUDIENCE: Do you think a revolution was averted in 1933 by FDR's quick action to put work programs into effect?

CLARENCE MITCHELL: I would like to volunteer to answer that because I think we were on the verge of a revolution. I know enough about the impact of Communist efforts in this country during that period because I was a young man just coming out of college. My good wife is a graduate of the University of Pennsylvania and is a distinguished lawyer. We were young people in that period and I know that from what I was able to observe firsthand, we were on the verge of a revolution. Anybody who heard, for example, Governor Floyd Olson up in Minnesota saying, "If what we are seeing now is evidence of capitalism, I hope it goes right down to hell," would know that we were on the brink of an upheaval which probably would have destroyed this country as we know it. And I think Mr. Roosevelt, by the things that he was able to do, saved us from a revolution.

I also think that we had better watch our step right now because if we don't stop doing some of the things that are letting people go hungry, taking old people out of places where they can live and things of that sort, we might find ourselves in the same kind of condition that we faced back in the 1930s.

FRANK FREIDEL: I quite agree with Clarence Mitchell on one point, and that is that these people were saying these things. But I think, putting it in a little bit broader context—and I hate to disagree with you in entirety—the indication in the 1932 election was that almost no one voted for a third-party ticket. There was, of course, the great disturbance of Milo Reno and his Farmer's Holiday movement in the Middle West in the summer of 1933 and into 1934. But I'm happy to say that I think that while there were revolutionaries here and there, by and large the American people were quite a long way from a revolution. Certainly we would have had great disturbances and great difficulties if it hadn't been for the Roosevelt programs, but I don't think a revolution was really eminent.

CLARENCE MITCHELL: Actually, when I think of the speeches that I heard Huey Long make, when I think of Father Coughlin coming on the radio talking about the South, saying "the darkies are no longer singing in the cotton fields," when I think of all the rhetoricians who were out there stirring up the discontented, it certainly does not require any great stretch of the imagination, in my opinion, to realize that if Mr. Roosevelt hadn't done something to give people relief, we would have had more situations like those in which the farmers who were being faced with mortgage foreclosures on their homes stood in the way of sheriffs to prevent those sheriffs from executing orders. I think if something hadn't been done about that we would have seen an attempted revolution in this country.

RAPPORTEUR'S SUMMARY

DOUGLASS CATER: Winston Churchill said once in pushing a dessert away, "This pudding has no theme." One might have been tempted at times this afternoon to say that about the rich smorgasbord that we were served.

If I had one wish, I would wish that the organization of the conference had started the other way, from right to left. I think we would have provoked a much livelier debate as we went along if we had done so. But so be it.

I detected a somewhat lopsided emphasis in this afternoon's discussion, given the title, "The Effect of the New Deal to the Present Time," on the persons rather than the substance of the New Deal. There seemed to me a bit of avoidance of what is the substance of this New Deal that we are considering now—where it stands, where it's going, its place in the politics of our time. And yet I would not have dismissed for a moment the wonderful summations on leaders and leaderships. Let me just remind you of a few.

First, from James Roosevelt, on leadership: "The courage to be hated"—what a great courage that is. From Truman: "Heroes know when to die." About LBJ: "Roosevelt without a Harvard education." About Franklin Roosevelt: "The one person who was never afraid." And I do think the cogitations this afternoon about the nature of fear in public life and how the leader has to lead in combating that fear of fear itself is something that is a tradition and that needs to be hearkened to.

I was not much elated by the quotation from Bill Moyers that LBJ's relationship to FDR was like that of Plato to Socrates. Somehow that one did not grab me. I think the statement that Eisenhower made the New Deal permanent is well worth pondering.

Finally, just as I was about to say that we really had not raised many questions of substance and that we particularly had not answered the question raised many, many years ago by John Adams when he said despairingly, "The art of governing has not advanced an inch since the time of Darius," we had the reminder from Mr. Clarence Mitchell that in the area of equality, we do have some lessons to ponder, that the evolution of the leadership consciousness and a public consciousness toward the inferior treatment of races is something that substantially has changed in America.

And yet I would remind you of one thing, Mr. Mitchell, as you were saying all that—and certainly working for Mr. Johnson, I would echo most of what you said—it was the Supreme Court, too, those nine old men, who set the terms of the debate. So in that case, it was not all political leadership that led to the evolution of race relations in America.

CLARENCE MITCHELL: I suffered because of the time restrictions, but I happen to be the author of an article which appeared in the *University of Nebraska Law Review* about the role of the Supreme Court with respect to the same thing, so I share your view.

DOUGLASS CATER: The question has kept echoing throughout the day: What is meant by, "Are we our brother's keeper?" Does it mean the welfare state or, at the other end of the pole, does it mean that we each hand a bowl of soup to our brother when we see he is hungry? I think it is a significant question to be raised. It has all sorts of ramifications which can be raised tomorrow when Mr. Brademas addresses the issue of education and education equality in America and the evolution from the New Deal to the Fair Deal to the New Frontier to the Great Society.

So there is a lot left to talk about in this conference. I think we've stirred the pot pretty good, but we've got another half day of hard work ahead of us.

Pickle

Ford

Brademas

Cater

Jordan

Kemp

Keyserling

Pepper

Rusher

Peterson

Randolph

IV

THE NEW DEAL'S LEGACY FOR THE FUTURE

J.J. PICKLE
GERALD R. FORD
JOHN BRADEMAS
DOUGLASS CATER
VERNON E. JORDAN, JR.
JACK F. KEMP
MARY DUBLIN KEYSERLING
CLAUDE D. PEPPER
WILLIAM RUSHER
ESTHER PETERSON
JENNINGS RANDOLPH

INTRODUCTION OF SPEAKER

J.J. (JAKE) PICKLE: When my good friend and colleague Gerald Ford became the thirty-eighth President of the United States, the entire House of Representatives, Democrats and Republicans alike, arose in unanimous and prideful salute to this able and trusted friend. For twenty-five years he had worked among us. We respected him, we loved him, and we trusted him. He was a man who kept his word.

Now, in the world of politics, keeping a man's word perhaps has more meaning than almost any profession. Gerald Ford kept his word. He was always fair, efficient, progressive, and courageous. As President, he came to us at the right time in American history.

Gerald Ford, as President, restored the confidence of the American people in their government. We shall always be grateful to him for that. How appropriate that he should be here with us today as we discuss the legacy of another President who led his country in a national crisis. He is one of the most distinguished, courageous, and outstanding Presidents who ever served us. I'm proud to present to you the Honorable Gerald Ford.

A PRESIDENT'S VIEW OF THE NEW DEAL

GERALD R. FORD

As a great Democratic former Speaker would say at the outset of his comments, it's a very high honor and a very great privilege to have the opportunity of being a part of this symposium with so many uniquely qualified individuals to assess the effects, both beneficial and detrimental, of the legacy of the New Deal.

Being only nineteen years old in 1932, I was not eligible to vote in the presidential election November 8th between Herbert Hoover and Franklin D. Roosevelt. At that time I was a struggling sophomore at the University of Michigan, both on election day and on March 4, 1933, when Franklin Delano Roosevelt took the oath of office.

As I look around this gathering this morning, I see that there aren't too many of you who were adults on these memorable dates in the political history of the United States.

My assessment of the New Deal over the past fifty years is predicated on very personal experiences in three distinct periods in my own lifetime: first, the period from 1931 to Pearl Harbor; second, from Pearl Harbor to 1948; and finally, my involvement in the political arena at the national level from 1948 to 1977. In the process of reviewing the New Deal's influence during these various time frames over the past half century, I found that my opinions, at least, have not been frozen.

I recall the stock market crash in 1929 and saw firsthand the terrible impact of the Depression on my own family and the families of my schoolmates, with unemployment at 25 percent in 1933. As house manager of my fraternity that year, I vividly recall the shock when overnight every bank in the state of Michigan was closed on February 10th.

Visualize, if you would, the impact in the state of Texas today if every bank were closed overnight.

How to feed forty-five fraternity brothers and personally how to rescue my slim bank account of less than $100 presented a somewhat considerable challenge. At that time on the Michigan campus, no student could anticipate being rescued by a check from a federal scholarship or a federal grant. There was none available.

In this era, I still remember the distressing clashes between Ford and General Motors over the unionization of their employees. The Battle of the Overpass at Ford and the sit-ins at General Motors were tragically very, very bloody conflicts. At this stage of my life, despite my upbringing as a solid Republican, I felt that something had gone wrong in America. My dear stepfather, when I would argue that the excesses of the 1920s had precipitated our nation's miseries and maybe the New Deal was the answer, would allege I was being terribly misled by those liberal, ivory-towered professors on the Michigan campus.

It was obvious to me then, and still is, that in the late 1920s and early 1930s, certain fundamental segments of our domestic economy had serious problems that needed regulation and new approaches. Although I never embraced all that FDR did in this particular period, I did applaud his efforts to unravel the devastations of the Smoot-Hawley tariff legislation under the leadership of Cordell Hull, his support of legislation to establish the Federal Deposit Insurance Corporation, his recognition that America's agriculture needed basic regulation to prevent the bankruptcy of our farmers, his support for new legislation in the area of labor management legislation, and his recommendations to regulate Wall Street with the Securities and Exchange Commission (SEC).

On review in 1983, fifty years later, my assessment is that the Roosevelt Administration moved necessarily with legislative proposals that were dramatic, and some would say radical, to meet the national crisis. There was, obviously, during this time span a wide swing of the political pendulum. It was the beginning of a much more activist federal government with significant increases in government regulation, by law as well as by executive mandate.

In the 1930s the United States tilted toward isolationism. Unquestionably, that was the prevailing attitude in the Middle West. As a product of this particular environment, I was critical of what I perceived to be the gradual shift of the Roosevelt Administration to one more concerned with America's role in foreign affairs, especially the problems created in Europe by Hitler. In retrospect, knowing what I know now, I was naive and uninformed. Perhaps that can be excused as a luxury of youth, when one has no responsibility for the fate of a nation, its people, or its principles.

In looking back to the late thirties and early forties, I have come to the conclusion—probably influenced by White House experiences—that FDR skillfully managed the shift of the United States from an isolated nonparticipant to a full partner, if not leader, in the worldwide struggle against aggression and oppression.

I'm reasonably familiar with all of the allegations—that President Roosevelt connived, that he made mistakes, and that he otherwise did a bad job in the very delicate negotiations and confrontations in the months leading up to December 7, 1941. I do not join in this chorus. Admittedly, as I said a moment ago, my view is prejudiced by two-and-a-half years in the White House.

Mr. Roosevelt, before Pearl Harbor, was dealing with a hesitant Congress and had no overwhelming public support for a more militant United States policy. The FDR legacy on these monumental decisions, in my judgment, looks better and better with the passing of time.

Pearl Harbor had a very major impact on my own life. The four years in naval service—a good share of it in the Pacific Basin—revised my views, as it did millions of others in the United States. We recognized that when the battles were real and lives were being lost, there had to be strong leadership in the White House, that the executive branch of the federal government had to be the dominant branch in our system of coequal coordinate branches, and that 531 members of the House and Senate had to play a secondary role.

Before some of you start to challenge 531, Alaska and Hawaii were not members of the United States, and we still had 435 members of the House.

Again, on reflection, one must come to the conclusion that FDR was a strong and effective wartime President. There are many who applaud Roosevelt's wartime leadership but who, on the other hand, bitterly criticize his diplomatic dealings with the Soviet Union as the European war came to an end. Critics allege FDR was in failing health at Yalta and Potsdam and, as a result, made bad deals that gave away too much to Stalin. The accuracy of these charges is controversial. Right or wrong, the fact that historians write pro and con dims the diplomatic legacy of President Roosevelt in this period.

My own foreign policy views, as a result of World War II, took a drastic shift from a typical midwestern isolationist to a broad-based internationalist. In all honesty, I became a Vandenberg Republican in foreign policy, with very strong views in support of the new role of the United States in global politics.

Although much of this shift in United States foreign policy came at the tail end of the Roosevelt Administration and in the early days of the Truman Administration, it was a change that had its genesis under FDR. For this redirection of America's global role, historians will write favorably of the New Deal.

Now, if I might, I would like to step back and review the legacy of the New Deal, primarily domestically, based on my own personal experiences in the legislative and executive branches from January 3, 1949, to January 20, 1977.

As I said earlier, the political pendulum that moved to the liberal part of the spectrum, based on the 1932 and '34 elections, resulted in significant legislative changes in the nation's capital. Most of the new laws emphasized the role of the central government in Washington, D.C. New programs, such as Social Security, were initiated to provide a base income for retirees. New commissions were established, such as the SEC to oversee and regulate Wall Street. The National Labor Relations Board (NLRB), under the Wagner Act, was born to monitor labor-management difficulties and controversies. Unemployment insurance and Workmen's Compensation became a reality, as did the minimum wage. The airlines and trucking industries underwent federal regulation by the Civil Aeronautics Board (CAB) and the Interstate Commerce Commission (ICC). The banking industry ended up with the Federal Deposit Insurance Corporation (FDIC) and other regulatory reforms.

The surge of such legislation in the late 1930s, which is the hallmark of the New Deal, continued to a lesser degree in the post-World War II period in the Truman and Kennedy Administrations. The trend was accelerated in 1964, '65, and '66 under President Johnson's Great Society initiatives. All of these Democratic Presidents and Democratic-controlled Congresses built on the legacy of the New Deal under FDR and were proud to do so.

Now, at some point following the 1968 presidential election—and I'm not wise enough to pinpoint with precision the exact time—there began a shift in public sentiment away from the New Deal concept that centralization of authority in the nation's capital and governmental regulation of our society was the answer to our problems and the means to a better life for all Americans. It may have been caused by citizen disillusionment with Washington leadership in the handling of the Vietnam War. It may have resulted from legislation or executive regulation going far too far in the penetration of our daily lives.

Whatever the cause, the political pendulum began to swing back from the heyday of the New Deal and others that followed that trend. Even a Democrat, Jimmy Carter, in 1976, successfully belabored the excesses of Washington that had had their birth in the New Deal. In my Administration, I was joined in a major deregulation effort of the CAB and the ICC by Senator Edward Kennedy. These proposals bore fruit under Carter and Reagan for the airline and the trucking industries and, to a degree, for the railroads.

Don't get me wrong. I'm not saying that the New Deal legacy across the board is being shattered today. I am saying that as times and circumstances change and as political sentiment ebbs and flows, what was tried and found useful in a previous era can and should be reviewed and revised in another.

Much of the basic social legislation enacted by the New Deal is still on the books. In some cases, it has been updated. Social Security is a good illustration of a program that has undergone many legislative expansions, revisions, and now probably a compromise to save it from bankruptcy. Labor-management legislation has gone through a series of changes from the Wagner Act to the Taft-Hartley Act to the Landrum-Griffin Act. The New Deal legacy that there should be laws regulating industrial relations is still valid. But the justification for the Wagner Act in the 1930s, as then enacted, did not exist in the forties and does not exist today.

This updating of legislation in no way degrades the legacy of the New Deal in this important area of our society. It simply illustrates that with the passage of time, we need new tools to deal with current problems. It also illustrates, in my judgment, the genius of the flexibility of our governmental system.

In the time allotted, there was no way that I could give you an in-depth analysis of the New Deal. I have, however, sought to give you personal reflections and to make the point that our viewpoints do change as our lifetime experiences give us new perspectives. Furthermore, under our system of government, thank goodness we have the capacity to hold on to fundamental developments, such as many of those initiated by the New Deal, yet to adjust them to resolve the new circumstances that confront us.

One final comment on FDR and his legacy. As one steps back and looks at the nation's problems during his term in the White House, one sees that there were monumental crises at home and abroad—a depression and a global military conflict. Our nation in those desperate days needed a leader who would stimulate the spirit of our people to meet the awesome challenges domestically as well as internationally. President Roosevelt, regardless of one's views on legislative programs and policies, had a tremendous talent to swing public opinion. In those crises, FDR did restore our faith in America. He did convince his fellow countrymen with his fantastic skill that we, as a nation, had the tools and the will to whip our economic problems at home and the aggressors abroad.

FDR's greatest contribution, his legacy that will stand the test of time, was his unquestioned talent to rekindle our spirit in times of despair. With that spirit, America did meet its challenges, and today we are the beneficiaries.

INTRODUCTION OF SPEAKER

JAKE PICKLE: John Brademas is easily one of the most learned men ever to serve in Congress. He will be especially remembered for his leadership in education and the arts. As a member of the House Education and Labor Committee, he advanced many of the education bills of our great education President, Lyndon Johnson. Just as LBJ was the education President, John Brademas was the chairman that advanced those bills and allowed them to become the law.

As the House Majority Whip, he was the third most powerful man in the United States Congress. Although he left Congress four years ago to become president of New York University, where his performance, as usual, has been in the summa cum laude category, John Brademas is remembered as a leader of the education bills in Congress, and history will record him as one of the key individuals in the movement to reform education in this country.

I am happy to present to you my dear friend John Brademas.

THE EDUCATION DIMENSION OF THE NEW DEAL LEGACY

JOHN BRADEMAS

The only time I ever saw President Franklin Roosevelt in person was over forty-seven years ago when I was a schoolboy of eight. He was in an open car that passed directly in front of my house at 701 North Michigan Street in South Bend, Indiana, on his way to th University of Notre Dame, where he was awarded an honorary degree. My entire family, enthusiastic partisans of FDR, waved from our front porch as the man we idolized drove by.

. Few leaders in the history of any nation have had so deep or such personal impact on the lives of so many as Franklin D. Roosevelt. I am sure you have listened with great fascination, as did I, to what I felt were the moving and eloquent words of President Ford as he talked about the impact of President Roosevelt on his own life and distinguished career.

One of the participants in this week's discussions, Professor William Leuchtenburg, recently gave us an example of how potent and direct this impact could be. He found evidence of a couple who, in 1928, had christened their newborn son Herbert Hoover Jones. Four years later they petitioned the courts, "desiring to relieve the young man from mortification, which he is suffering and will suffer," and asked that his name be changed to Franklin D. Roosevelt Jones.

We are here today to discuss the legacy of the New Deal and what it means for the future. As I reflected on the meaning of President Roosevelt and the New Deal in my own life, I realized that we were to meet on the campus of a great university, and, moreover, realized that we were to do so in a building dedicated to the memory of America's "education President," Lyndon B. Johnson. I decided that the most useful contribution I could make to our discussions would be to focus on one particular theme, that of education.

Beyond these reasons, I believe that we can find in Roosevelt's views and policies on education the larger leitmotifs of his political philosophy: the promise of equality of opportunity, the importance of peaceful social change, and a view of government as a positive force for the people whom it serves.

So I should like to talk about the education dimension of the New Deal legacy: first, to illustrate from my own experience as a member of Congress the ongoing influence of the Rooseveltian heritage; and second, to illuminate the broader message of the New Deal for the future of our country.

Let me at the outset say something of Franklin Roosevelt's attitude toward education. What comes through clearly in his statements and speeches is his sense of the relationship between education and three other elements: economic well-being, democratic values, and individual opportunity. Roosevelt thought education vital to the revival of the economic life of the nation. In a speech before the National Education Association midway in his second term, he asserted, "The only real capital of a nation is its natural resources and its human beings. So long as we take care of and make the most of them, we shall survive as a strong nation.... If we skimp on that capital, if we exhaust our natural resources and weaken the capacity of our human beings, then we shall go the way of all weak nations." The human as well as physical capital of the country was to be conserved and reconstructed by the New Deal.

Education was also in Roosevelt's eyes the safeguard of the American way of governing, of democracy. For he said, "Democracy cannot succeed unless those who express their choice are prepared to choose wisely. Upon our educational system," he said, "must largely depend the perpetuity of those institutions upon which our freedom and our security rest."

Yet, as FDR looked about him in the 1930s, he saw that opportunity for the education he deemed essential to the American democracy was not at all equal. In words that foreshadowed the legislation of which Lyndon Johnson was most proud, the Elementary and Secondary Education Act of 1965, Roosevelt said, just a quarter of a century earlier:

> No American child, merely because he happens to be born where property values are low and where local taxes do not, even though they should, support the schools should be

placed at a disadvantage in his preparation for citizenship.

There is probably a wider divergence today in the standard of education than there was a hundred years ago; it is, therefore, our immediate task to seek to close that gap.

But Roosevelt did not directly attack this problem. Fears over federal control of schools, misgivings over spending more public dollars during a depression, and, especially, the specter of the church-state conflict—all these factors dictated a more subtle approach. And so FDR promised no large-scale program of federal aid to education. He spoke rather of "entering wedges," which, he told a group of visiting state school superintendents at the White House in 1935, "are comparatively small so far as the total expenditure of money goes. But looking at the problems as a whole, we are gradually working, I think, toward a greater national interest and understanding in the great many things that the national government can properly do."

The first of the wedges appeared with New Deal programs we do not normally associate with education: public works, conservation projects, and youth training. In December 1933, the Federal Emergency Relief Administration provided what was then called "work-aid" to students and relief funds to teachers to keep schools open which would otherwise have had to close their doors. In addition, thousands of young people who enrolled in the Civilian Conservation Corps (CCC) received instruction in the basic skills of reading, writing, and arithmetic and were offered vocational and academic courses at levels ranging from elementary to high school. The National Youth Administration, which focused on vocational training and jobs, meant, for thousands of young men and women, enough money to finance their high school and college educations. And within a year of the start of the NYA in 1935, some 400,000 students were working under its auspices.

Again, if I may quote Professor Leuchtenburg, he reminds us of some of those who benefited from this program during the Depression era:

At the University of Michigan, the NYA gave a job—that of feeding mice—to one of its undergraduates who was an aspiring playwright, Arthur Miller. Roosevelt put in charge of the NYA for the entire State of Texas, a 27-year-old former congressional assistant, Lyndon Johnson. Johnson later remembered that one NYA job had gone to the son of a sharecropper who had come without a dollar in his pocket to work his way through the University of Texas, John Connally. And in North Carolina, NYA employed, at 35 cents an hour, a Duke University law student, Richard Nixon.

Through these and other programs, money was funneled into aid to students and teachers, construction of classrooms, and adult education. The Works Projects Administration not only put people to work building dams, highways, and parks, but employed others in playhouses, concert halls, and studios. Through the WPA, as Mr. Houseman movingly reminded us last night, hundreds of writers, artists, dancers, and musicians— whose talents might otherwise have been lost—gave new impetus to the American mind and the American imagination. I here cite but three such brightly shining names—Saul Bellow, Jackson Pollock, and Walker Evans—and I add only that I remember still, as a schoolboy, Sunday nights in South Bend's Leeper Park, where local musicians played open-air concerts, another WPA enterprise.

So although Roosevelt was President at a time when, for reasons I have suggested, no major direct federal role for education was politically possible, he understood the importance of education to the nation's life and future. If not a dominant strain, support for education was nonetheless woven into the pattern of the New Deal in programs like the NYA, the CCC, and the WPA.

The Second World War struck these "entering wedges" like a hammer and opened the way for the largest direct program of federal support for education in the nation's history. Ever the pragmatic politician, propelled both by the economic impact of returning veterans and by the political muscle of the American Legion, Roosevelt supported and signed into law the GI Bill of Rights, under which the national government paid for the education of millions of young Americans. In terms of the numbers of persons receiving aid, the amount of money spent, and the impact on the nation's educational standards, the World War II GI Bill was the most sweeping and significant federal education program ever enacted. With its passage and its demonstration that financial assistance from the federal government did not bring loss of local control, the stage was set for expansion of the federal role in education.

Like many of you, I was a direct beneficiary of the GI Bill. With its help, I went at the age of nineteen to Harvard, where, by the way, I met another participant in today's proceedings, Doug Cater. That Doug and I lived in the same building—now known as Adams House—as FDR had at Harvard was a daily reminder of the Rooseveltian heritage. More important, what I learned in Cambridge reinforced my social and political values: I was a Roosevelt Democrat.

After Harvard I went on to Oxford as a Rhodes Scholar. At both institutions, I reveled in the opportunity to study under gifted teachers and to talk long into the night with the bright, intense students of the postwar generation.

The experiences of those years not only enriched my own life but impressed upon me the importance of education, especially as a ladder to social and economic advancement. That the son of a Greek immigrant and a Hoosier schoolteacher should have been able to study at the two finest universities in the world dramatized for me the significance of an opportunity for education.

From England, I went back home to South Bend and six months later, in 1954, I ran for Congress. I was defeated—but, President Ford, by only half a percent.

While I waited for the tide to turn, I joined, as assistant in charge of research on issues, the presidential campaign staff of Adlai Stevenson, which is where I first met a number of the people in this room. And here, once more, I was to feel the force of the Roosevelt legacy. One need only read the speeches and position papers in the national campaigns of Adlai Stevenson to see how effectively he laid the groundwork for much of John F. Kennedy's New Frontier and Lyndon Johnson's Great Society, and especially their policies on education.

In a 1955 speech entitled, "Education: A National Cause," Stevenson urged adoption of a program of federal aid for school construction and teacher training, for college scholarships and loans, for foreign educational exchanges, as well as for the expansion of vocational and adult education. Here, in words that were direct echoes of Roosevelt's rhetoric a decade and a half before, was what Adlai Stevenson said in Chicago as he spoke to the National Education Association. He said, "We have reached a point where the financing of education, as distinguished from its control, can no longer be taken care of entirely from local or even state and local revenues. . . . Some measure of assistance to public education from the federal purse has now become necessary."

The year 1956 disappointed not only Adlai Stevenson's presidential ambitions but my congressional aspirations. In 1958, however, on my third try, I was at long last elected to Congress, where, until the wicked rebellion of 1980, I served for twenty-two years.

I must tell you that even before I set off from Indiana for Washington twenty-five years ago, I determined to get involved in education. Now, as you all know, the most important decision of a newly elected Congressman is his committee assignment. Having first won election in 1958, the year the National Defense Education Act became law, I felt strongly that the time had come for the federal government to provide greater support for education in the United States. And that, of course, was the year after the Soviets had launched the first Sputnik and shocked Americans into a reevaluation of the state of education in our country. It seemed to me that the best way to play a part in what I concluded would be a burgeoning federal role in education was to become a member of the Education and Labor Committee of the House.

A few days after the 1958 election, at the urging of someone known to many of you, my friend, the late D. B. Hardeman, I telephoned the then Speaker, Mr. Rayburn, who lived in a small town about 250 miles north and east of here. I flew to Dallas, rented a car, and drove up to Bonham to call on the Speaker, who lived in a white frame house just off the side of the road.

After lunch, sitting in a rocker in his living room, Speaker Rayburn said to me, with blunt friendliness, "I s'pose you want to talk about your committee?"

"Yes, sir," I told him. "Mr. Speaker, I would like to be on the Education and Labor Committee."

"Hazardous committee, hazardous committee," the Speaker replied.

I said I realized that but that I felt it was an important assignment, nonetheless, because the issues that committee would be considering would have a major impact on the people I represented in Northern Indiana and, moreover, that in the years ahead, the national government would be giving much more attention to education.

Speaker Rayburn was not in the habit of issuing guarantees to freshman Congressmen and there were forty-eight new Democrats elected to the House that year. But when committees were named, I drew my first choice, Education and Labor, and I remained on that committee throughout my service in Congress.

In fact, the seat I came to hold, as second-ranking member of the Elementary and Secondary Education Subcommittee, was previously held by a Massachusetts member who had left the House to win a seat in the Senate, and in two years would be headed for still higher office. That man, of course, was President Kennedy.

As President, John Kennedy was a vigorous advocate of increased federal support for education. Although his aspirations for a general school aid bill were frustrated during his Administration, his legacy includes several bills President Johnson signed into law in the weeks after the assassination: measures for medical and dental education, college academic facilities, and vocational education.

In his ringing assertion that "education is the keystone in the arch of freedom and progress," John F. Kennedy sounded a Rooseveltian theme at the same time he set the stage for the midsixties and the explosion of educational legislation that was to come.

For me personally, the opportunity as a member of that committee of the House of Representatives to have taken part in the process of expanding federal support for education was the most gratifying part of my own service in Congress. For during these years, I had the privilege of helping advance the legacy of Franklin Roosevelt, of Adlai Stevenson, and of John F. Kennedy, through sponsoring and helping write a spectrum of bills to support the schools and libraries, colleges and universities, and other institutions of learning and culture in our country.

But as you and I know, the most prodigious outpouring of such legislation was to begin following the presidential and congressional elections of 1964, under the leadership of the man in whose memorial we gather today, Lyndon Baines Johnson.

Many of you have heard the story told by my friend and the distinguished Majority Leader, Jim Wright, of that special election in the Tenth Congressional District of Texas in 1937, to fill a vacancy created by the death of the incumbent. There were nearly half a dozen candidates, if not more, and one of them declared, "I'm for Franklin Roosevelt and I am for everything he's trying to do." That one was elected, and his name was Lyndon Johnson.

Thirty years after the arrival of that freshman Congressman from Texas—whose seat, by the way, continues to be splendidly filled by Jake Pickle—a policy of major federal support for education was finally established. During the years of President Johnson, Congress authorized an unprecedented array of education programs.

I recall, Mrs. Johnson, when I was here for the dedication of this marvelous library in 1971, how the President greeted me after the ceremonies. He had, I recall, a grandchild—whether it was Lyn Nugent or Lucinda Robb, I really don't recall—perched on his shoulder.

He said, "John, I want you to go up to the eighth floor"— he was referring to a suite adjacent to the replica of the Oval Office— "and look at that table with the pens I used to sign all those education bills you and I wrote."

I did look, and there were thirty pens there.

So allow me today, very briefly, to speak to you about what we in Washington tried to do to support education and the activities of the mind and the imagination during the years of my own service in the nation's capital.

First, we made—and when I say "we," I include Presidents, Senators, and Representatives of both parties—a commitment to make education accessible to those likely to be excluded. Most obviously, I think here of the Elementary and Secondary Education Act of '65, which, for the first time, provided substantial federal funds to help our grade schools and high schools. In signing that measure, outside the former one-room school house at Stonewall, Texas, where he first attended class, President Johnson declared, "I believe deeply that no law I have signed or will ever sign means more to the future of America."

I think as well of Head Start, the Job Corps, the Neighborhood Youth Corps, Upward Bound, and all the other components of

President Johnson's War on Poverty. I think of the vocational and manpower training programs, as well as one on which I labored long with my Republican colleague, Al Quie of Minnesota—the Education for All Handicapped Children Act.

And to assure access to a college education in this country, Presidents of both parties—Presidents Eisenhower, Kennedy, Johnson, Nixon, Ford, and Carter—as well as Democrats and Republicans in Congress, created from the National Defense Education Act of '58, through a series of higher education laws, a fabric of grants, loans, and work-study jobs for talented and motivated but needy young men and women.

We made a second commitment during my time in Washington—to support our institutions of culture. You all know the milestones along this path: the establishment, at President Johnson's initiative, of the National Endowments for the Arts and the Humanities, as well as programs to help public libraries and school and college libraries. I was proud to have been a champion of all of these measures on Capitol Hill and over the years to have initiated some measures of my own, such as assistance for museums of every kind.

There was a third commitment—to strengthen international studies and research in our colleges and universities. And here again, I was glad to have carried LBJ's banner, working with Doug Cater, as principal sponsor in Congress of the International Education Act of 1966, as well as of other efforts to encourage teaching and learning about other peoples and cultures.

Yet a fourth commitment was to research. I note here the crucial role of the national government in enhancing our understanding of ourselves and our universe through, among other entities, the National Science Foundation, the National Institutes of Health, and the National Institute of Education.

Let me reiterate that all these commitments were made in a spirit of bipartisanship. It was President Eisenhower who urged the National Defense Education Act, which declared that "no student of ability will be denied an opportunity for higher education because of financial need."

It was President Nixon who, in his 1970 Higher Education Message to Congress, asserted that "no qualified student who wants to go to college should be barred by lack of money."

The very first major piece of legislation Gerald Ford signed as

President was an omnibus education act authorizing funds for virtually every federal program to aid elementary and secondary schools. "Throughout our history," President Ford declared in 1976, "federal encouragement and assistance to education has been an essential part of the American system. To abandon it now would be to ignore the past and to threaten the future."

In 1980 President Carter would declare on signing the Middle Income Student Assistance Act: "We've brought college within the reach of every student in this nation who's qualified for higher education. The idea that lack of money should be no barrier to a college education is no longer a dream; it's a reality."

I shall not here detail the gains from this effort over the last quarter of a century on behalf of education. But I can observe that the proportion of blacks with a high school diploma more than doubled, from 20 percent to over 50 percent, between 1960 and 1980; that during those years the nation's college enrollments rose from 3.6 million to over 11 million; that federal research dollars led to life-saving advances in fighting disease; and that federal funds for the arts and humanities stimulated cultural activities in every state in the union.

In all these achievements—and I have touched on only a few—the legacy of the New Deal has been increasingly realized, under Presidents of both of our great political parties, until 1981. Since then, we have had an Administration which has been pressing a profound and fundamental shift in federal policy toward the institutions of learning and culture in American life. The Administration of Ronald Reagan has been attempting to reverse nearly all of the national and bipartisan commitments of which I have spoken. For there can be no doubt that the Reagan Administration has leveled a steady and systematic assault on American education at every level.

A report recently issued by the nonpartisan Urban Institute entitled "The Reagan Experiment" concludes that by the time the Administration's planned cutbacks take full effect in 1984, federal funds for elementary, secondary, and vocational education will be about half of what they were in 1981. The Administration has been particularly intent on destroying or weakening programs for children from low-income families, as well as efforts for the education of handicapped children.

In respect to the diversity of measures my colleagues and I, both

Democrats and Republicans, shaped over nearly twenty-five years to help students who needed help to go to college, President Reagan in each of his budgets has taken the ax and whacked away. Last year he even tried to eliminate graduate students from eligibility for guaranteed loans. And this year, as I read the President's higher education budget, all I can say is, "There he goes again!"

Last month in New York, I served as an honorary pallbearer in the Cathedral of St. John the Divine in tribute to that tireless and effective advocate of the arts in our country, Nancy Hanks. I found myself in the same procession with former President Nixon, who appointed Nancy chairman of the Arts Endowment and who consistently supported increased funds for the arts and humanities even as did President Ford.

But President Reagan, by way of contrast, is the first President of either party to attempt to reduce the budgets of the Endowments and simply eliminate other programs that assist museums and libraries.

You will not be surprised to hear me say that I am heartened to observe, in the face of such systematic attacks, the reforging of the historic bipartisan coalition in Congress in support of education and the arts. In the stiffening resistance the Reagan proposals are meeting, I see evidence of the ongoing strength of a tradition that really took root in our country in the years of President Roosevelt. And if I may offer an ex-politician's prediction, I venture to suggest that because so widespread among the American people is support of education—and concretely of the kinds of federal programs of which I have spoken—and because President Reagan is the first President of either party in the last generation to attempt to cripple that support, education will be a highly visible issue in the presidential campaign of 1984. I think this will be true particularly if Mr. Reagan seeks reelection, but even if he does not.

Certainly most of the Democratic presidential contenders are making education, research, science, and technology important components of their speeches and proposals. And in their calls to increase our investment in human capital, we hear echoes of FDR a half-century earlier urging, in his words, the "conserving of the health, energy, skill, and morale of our population which will be the America of tomorrow."

There are other reasons for my suggesting that support for education is likely to be an important issue next year. One is its vital connection to the strength of our economy; another, its indispensable part in our national security. Beyond these—which ought to be enough—is yet another—the desire of Americans to improve their own lives and those of their children. This, of course, is the motivation that gave birth and direction to the New Deal and carried forward its impulses even until today.

And so the legacy of the New Deal for the American future is, I think, threefold. One part speaks to the quantitative and qualitative dimensions of our lives: health and housing, jobs and food, education and fair treatment for all. A second aspect of the heritage touches on the way we conduct politics in this country. The New Deal was a triumph of pragmatism over ideology, of flexibility over fanaticism. The Roosevelt era, moreover, demonstrated that in the face of terrible times, government could be an instrument for peaceful and democratic social change.

A third contribution of the New Deal legacy is the demonstration that government need not be the enemy of the people but can, indeed should, be their servant. Many people today pay lip service to the notion that government should "get off our backs." Yet, very few want government out of their lives when it comes to measures that directly benefit them.

Even today, at a time of deep recession and the highest unemployment in forty years, the most antigovernment rhetorician of them all, Ronald Reagan, proclaimed in his State of the Union message a few weeks ago, "We who are in government must take the lead in restoring the economy."

Now, Mr. Chairman, I said at the outset of these remarks that I would talk both about the meaning of the New Deal for our country and about its impact on my own career as a legislator. Now that I am a university president, I apparently still cannot escape. Here are these words, spoken just over fifty years ago on the occasion of the celebration of its centennial by New York University:

> What impresses me most is that New York University is a positive and actual influence upon the lives of such a huge body of students. It has been and is a tremendous factor in educating not just the rich and the leisure class, but young

people in practically every walk of life. . . . In this it fits in with the true ideal of education in a democracy.

Those were the words spoken in 1931 by Governor Franklin D. Roosevelt of New York. And a half-century later, they remain true for us all.

PANEL PRESENTATIONS

DOUGLASS CATER, CHAIR: A fortnight ago in the splendid Gerald Ford Library in Ann Arbor, President Ford was host to a conference on citizenship education. He and President Jimmy Carter convened for the full period of the conference. They admitted that they had always liked each other, that we had been fooled when they pretended they had minor disagreements. It was a love feast.

President Carter said—and this is of interest in our attempts to define "leadership"—that sometimes he felt about his period like the man who had been hauled before the judge for being intoxicated and setting his bed on fire, and who pled, "Your Honor, I was drunk but that bed was on fire before I got in it."

I reminded you yesterday that one of the eloquent definitions of "leadership" was the courage to be hated, and I'm planning to fulfill that leadership role to the full this morning.

This is our last chance to get serious and to get at each other on measures of substance about the New Deal's legacy for the future. We all have our favorite anecdotes about FDR. Let's tell them but very, very briefly, if we have to. Let's mainly address ourselves to the topic.

My job is to try to provoke a discussion, not just a series of set pieces. And in order to do that, with this large a panel, we do have to get on with it so that then we can have at each other back and forth before we throw it open to you in the audience who may have questions or concerns. I have to get you to the church on time.

VERNON JORDAN: I recognize the New Deal as the beginning of compassionate government in our nation. I recognize it as the beginning of necessary government restraint on unbridled free enterprise activity. I recognize the New Deal as having dealt with very basic bread-and-butter issues of the nation. And I recognize the New Deal as the forerunner of the Great Society.

I am to some extent a beneficiary of the New Deal. I grew up in Atlanta in the first public housing project for then "colored" people in the country. My oldest brother was in the CCC camp. I grew up with the legacy of FDR. Whenever I went to rural places in the South as a little boy, there were always in those roadside shanties pictures of FDR and Jesus. And so he has been very much a part of my life.

But I also have to remember that when I was in the sixth grade, in 1941, in an old, segregated, dilapidated, ill-equipped double-sessioned school, I used a primer that had been used ten years before by a white student at a better school in another part of town.

I do have to remember that at the same time the New Deal was being inaugurated, lynching was a Saturday night activity and entertainment in some parts of the country.

I do remember that my mother and father could not register to vote in the primaries in Georgia until 1944. The New Deal started in 1933.

I do remember that in World War II we had to set up a special training camp for black flyers at Tuskegee, and that we fought that war in segregated armies.

So as I look at the New Deal—and I understand philosophically all of its meaning—I also understand that the New Deal operated within the context of *Plessy* versus *Ferguson*, that even the soup lines were segregated, and that during the New Deal we were second-class citizens and also second-class beneficiaries.

I was very impressed with John Brademas's talking about Connally and Nixon going to the University of Texas and to Duke University. That was not possible for young black men and women. Barbara and I could not have come here when John Connally did, for only one reason, and that was race.

I do not want to sound irreverent. I do not want to appear not to fully appreciate the social and governmental consequences of the New Deal. But it is clear to me that it was a very hard time for some people in this country, and the basic aspects of the New Deal did not address themselves to that predicament.

JACK KEMP: The historical perspective that President Ford put on the legacy of Franklin Roosevelt and members of his party, including President Johnson, is an important contribution to not only this particular debate but the whole realm of government policy and economic policy and international policy in America in this last third of the twentieth century.

Let me be direct. I'm glad Vernon started off with a historical perspective as it relates to his own personal life and that of his family and that of his race—that all of us have come a long way and we still have a long way to go.

I can't tell any anecdotes about Franklin Roosevelt because I wasn't even born in 1932 or '33. My parents were Republicans, Wendell Willkie Republicans, whatever that was, in the 1940s. So I grew up as a teenager wondering about Franklin Roosevelt. Only through the history books have I had an opportunity to learn about Franklin Roosevelt. I have read *The American Experiment*, by James McGregor Burns and William Manchester's book, *The Glory and the Dream*. But the book that had the greatest impact upon me is *FDR's Last Year, April 1944-April 1945* by Jim Bishop, which just literally, as an American, brought tears to my eyes and a chill to my spine, recognizing the charisma, the leadership. Franklin Roosevelt did for us what any great leader has to do for a people. In fact, there is no other reason for a political party than to provide that hope and that leadership. Franklin Roosevelt gave us that hope in terms of the debate over social justice and government policy and economics and international policy. Walter Lippmann said one time, "It is true that that government is best which governs least." He also said, "It is equally true that that government is best which does the most for people." The purpose of leadership is to bring into balance the role of government in people's lives and the ability of people to control their own lives.

And certainly social justice is not just the redistribution of wealth. Social justice is the removal of impediments to expanding the wealth. Part of wealth is physical; part of it is metaphysical. Part of it is material; part of it is spiritual. Part of it is capital; part of it is labor. Finally, part of wealth is tangible, and part of it, as John Brademas reminded us, is intangible—education and opportunity and the type of things this country has a commitment to, expanding for all people.

I'm glad that we're going to have a loving look at Franklin Roosevelt. John Gardner, during the Vietnam War, said, "America seems to be caught in a crossfire between the uncritical lovers and the unloving critics." It trivializes the memory of Franklin Roosevelt not to look at him in a critical way. You can still be loving and be critical in the historical sense.

So from that standpoint, I hope this panel will look favorably at the legacy of Franklin Roosevelt but that it will ultimately recognize that you can't help the poor by making the nation poor. You can only help the poor by making this nation richer—not just materially but in all those elements of capital of which John Brademas reminded us. This country is a lot more than just a safety net. As important as that is, it also has to provide a safety ladder so that every child of God can have the opportunity to become all that they were meant to be.

MARY KEYSERLING: It's a tough job to be asked to stick to one idea when you're talking about the New Deal legacy. I will speak about the essence of the New Deal spirit and philosophy which, in my opinion, is most important for today and for the future. The essence, in my judgment, was the building of human security, the assurance of freedom from want and freedom from fear. Government action was championed to meet human need, recognizing that when living standards are lifted, the whole country is strengthened.

I agree, Mr. Kemp, that we must strengthen the economy. But the essence of the New Deal was building living standards from the bottom. Said FDR in his first inaugural address, "Our greatest primary task is to put people to work." The programs that followed cut unemployment nearly in half within the first four New Deal years. Relief appropriations, WPA, CCC, Social Security (including unemployment compensation), minimum-wage and maximum-hour legislation, recognition of the importance of collective bargaining—these were sound investments, not just outright expenditures. For when human needs are met and purchasing power rises, goods get sold, employment accelerates, government revenues mount, and profits increase. Improve your income distribution from the bottom up.

This vital legacy of the New Deal was treasured in the Truman years. The annual rate of real economic growth averaged 4.9 percent, unemployment declined to less than 3 percent, and the annual rate of inflation averaged less than 3 percent, declining to less than 1 percent in the last year. And government budget surpluses far exceeded the deficits, which were tiny. Purchasing power was built from the bottom up.

In the Kennedy-Johnson years, too, the New Deal legacy that I have spoken of prevailed. These two great Presidents were also committed to human needs. Particularly do I want to pay tribute to President Johnson and his extraordinary leadership in lifting living standards and civil rights. I wish there were time to talk more about these gains.

The economy in the Johnson years grew again at the average annual rate of 4.9 percent, measured in constant dollars. Inflation and unemployment were low. Purchasing power rose very impressively. Most important, the median real income of our families rose 34 percent and poverty declined 45 percent in those eight years.

I am sorry to say I strongly believe that over the subsequent years, 1969 forward, the trickle-down economic approach has been substituted for the New Deal legacy. Today, I'm sorry to say the purchasing power—that is, wages in constant dollars— of the average weekly earnings of all workers in private employment is down to what it was in 1961, twenty-two years ago. This is the major cause of the serious recessions of recent years.

Median family income, also measured in constant dollars, has fallen substantially despite the rapid increase in the proportion of families with two-parent earners. I'm sorry to have to report that poverty increased 26 percent from '73 to '81, and the figures for '82 and '83 will be considerably higher. The poor are poorer, the rich are richer, and what a price we have paid.

Our factories are down to 67 percent utilization, and true unemployment has risen to over 14 million people, the highest actual number of jobless in our history. Consumer prices have nearly tripled, and the federal deficit has soared over this anti-New Deal legacy period. We have gone down the economic hill too far.

President Reagan paid tribute, yes, to FDR in his campaign. But what a pity that he isn't aware of the most vital elements of the New Deal legacy—concern for those who most need concern and willingness to invest in building living standards from the bottom up. As I have already said, this is an investment that quickly returns the cost—wages increase; tax receipts gain; and deficits diminish. The poor become less poor, and the richer don't get hurt; they get richer, too, but not quite as rich.

Lift the economy by cutting the taxes of the prosperous? No. Will that money be invested? It can't be. Will the automobile companies accept investors' money when plant utilization is down so low, and when it is down so low because purchasing power has shrunk?

I believe the country will have to come to understand these fundamentals of the New Deal legacy. And when they do, I believe that we will see an upturn that's consistent and strong.

I do believe that the legacy soon will again be recognized—in a little more than two years, if I may say so. It will be recognized because you students who are here, like the great majority of our people, are humane and caring, and the lessons of the New Deal will once again come into reality.

CLAUDE PEPPER: I'm very grateful for the privilege of being here on this occasion and having the opportunity to participate in recollections about one of the great eras of human history and our country.

The New Deal is not just a lot of houses that were built or a lot of jobs that were given or a lot of particular things that were done. The New Deal, in my opinion, epitomizes two things.

First, it reflects the concern of the government for the welfare of the people. Franklin D. Roosevelt—and I think all of us would want to include that great lady Eleanor Roosevelt in his accomplishments and contributions—was a man who, like the man who lived in a house by the side of the road, was a friend to man. He was concerned about the people of this country. In one of his addresses, he said, "I am determined that the welfare of every American shall be a subject of primary concern to the government of the United States."

No one was too small to be the subject of his concern and his compassion, and he brought that sense of compassion into the government of the United States. He reminded the American people that the Preamble of our Constitution said "we the people" founded the government of the United States, not anybody else.

He believed that the government, just because it happened to be located in Washington and was remote geographically from many of the people, should not be, in its concern, remote from the problems of the people. The federal government should not sit there like a knot on a log and be callous to people dying without medical care, children growing up without education, people living without decent homes about them, people lacking adequate nourishment, and the like. So the New Deal is primarily a principle, a principle of care and concern for the people of the United States, by the government of the United States.

The second aspect of the New Deal that I would emphasize is that it was not just a program to spend money or do this, that, and the other. The New Deal simply reflected a pragmatic, realistic approach to meeting the needs and the challenges of the people. It advocated the use in any reasonable and proper way of the power and function of government to help the people. Those are principles that are eternal. They apply in one generation to one set of facts and in another to another.

It may be the government is going to plant trees in arid lands swept by forceful winds blowing away the soil, to recapture America's agricultural productivity. Maybe in another case it's building a hospital or giving an artist a chance to paint a mural in the post office so he, too, can eat. It's the principle, I think, that's often overlooked.

So let us remember this principle: concern, legitimate care for the people, compassion even of a remote government for the well-being of all the people, privilege for no particular few but justice and equity for all. Let us also remember the application of the principle: reasonable, pragmatic programs to use, wherever right and proper, the government which belongs to the people to help the people. That, in my opinion, is the New Deal. It should, and I think it will, live forever.

WILLIAM RUSHER: When I talk about the New Deal, I am referring to the domestic policies of the New Deal. There was much more to Mr. Roosevelt's administrations, of course, but the New Deal was, I think, the domestic aspect of them. He himself said, toward the beginning of his third term, that Dr. New Deal had been replaced by Dr. Win the War.

There is no question that the central legacy of the New Deal for the future, however we assess the validity of it, is the belief in the desirability of government activism and in the efficacy of government intervention in the society at large.

I think that what has happened, as one might expect over fifty years, is that we have come along that road a long distance. I'm not sure it's altogether fair to Franklin Roosevelt to associate him with all of the government activism that has gone on since his death. In fact, while I reserve the right to be critical of this or that New Deal program, I think that a great deal of the problem of government activism is the result of the things that haven't occurred since he died.

We have seen that government can be ineffective in its efforts. It is one thing to declare, with the best will in the world, a war on poverty. It's quite another to win it.

We have seen that certain programs which were not only politically astute but seemed thoroughly compassionate, like food stamps, can be abused, and abused where the American people in their supermarket checkout lines can see it.

We can see that the government can be inefficient, so that there is a certain amount of justice to Milton Freidman's remark that if you put the government in charge of the Sahara Desert, within five years you would have a shortage of sand.

We must remember that as we speak of the need to appropriate greater and greater amounts of funds to these desirable programs, someone, somewhere along the line might rise and inquire who is going to be the source of these funds. They will ask because, my good young people, it is going to be the workers of America. That's where the wealth is and the only place it can come from.

I would close by suggesting simply this: Do not make the mistake of taking a past great experience and applying it too literally to what may not be the same problem. Do not believe that President Reagan, or anybody else today, is necessarily antagonistic to the fundamental objectives that we share just because his solutions are different. Maybe the problem is different.

Keep an eye, at any rate, on that possibility. And remember James Russell Lowell's remarks in his wonderful poem, "The Present Crisis in 1848," when he made that point, speaking of the attitude we have toward the pilgrim fathers:

> Yet we make their truth our falsehood,
> Thinking that hath made us free,
> Hoarding it in moldy parchments
> While our tender spirits flee
> The rude grass of that great impulse
> That drove them across the sea.

ESTHER PETERSON: I have a different base from all of you. I was a gym teacher when I first felt the excitement and the promise of the New Deal, which changed the direction that I wanted to go. I want to talk today about the legacy as it applies to "consumerism."

The development of consumer rights—the articulation of food safety standards and all of that—is an important part of it. Another part of the legacy is the establishment of the principle of consumer representation in decisionmaking—that consumers should have a say and be represented and be able to intervene in the economic decisions that affect their lives.

In the area of consumer rights, the New Deal, except for the Meat Inspection Act of 1906, was the first effort to build consumer safeguards into almost every facet of our American life. The Department of Agriculture was fertile ground for planning and experimenting. Other agencies expanded, addressing such needs as housing, credit, electrification, labeling, and family security. There was enthusiasm throughout the government and the morale was high. People in government were working to help the family not only to cope with disasters but to meet their needs in the marketplace for a better life.

In the area of consumer representation in decisionmaking, there was early recognition in the New Deal that the automatic working of the marketplace does not result in the public interest in policymaking, and that all parties affected should be represented. This means labor, business, farmers, and, yes, the consumer—the user of the results of production.

Consumers had a first taste of representation during the period the NRA was in effect. Mary Ramsey, the sister of Averell Harriman, was the first consumer representative, but her appointment was short-lived because the Supreme Court declared the unconstitutionality of the NRA in 1937.

Later, a consumer representative was established in the War Advisory Board. Martha Eliot held the position, and she had very tough sledding. The big boys in labor and industry and agriculture did not want a consumer representative and they very definitely did not want a woman. And they made it quite difficult for her.

For example, when she said she wanted an office like the others had, they said, "You mean to say you, a woman, a consumer representative, should have an office, an equal status on the Consumer Advisory Board along with General Motors and those?"

She was tough; she hung in.

The worst problem was that they used to meet a good deal in the dining room, and the dining room where they were housed was a stag room so she couldn't be in on those conferences. That was before they were integrated, of course.

Later, President Kennedy established the Consumer Advisory Committee, saying he felt that the roads to representation were certainly well covered by all the interests but the consumer. Then LBJ moved ahead and established the first Special Assistant for Consumer Affairs. And with his unparalleled legislative skills he pushed through massive new consumer laws—truth in packaging, truth in lending, and others. And then, of course, Nixon came and consumerism rested a bit, and the others came and it rested a bit.

And now where are we? I would say it's sad. Individuals in charge of administering the consumer laws don't believe in them. Orders are being revoked that were strung for our protection. Witness, for example, the revocation of the executive order on the control of the exportation of hazardous substances and note the special-interest exemptions to the antitrust laws.

Jancolovich says that consumers feel left out now in the government decisionmaking. Lou Harris, in a recent poll, said that consumers are stirring as individuals, although the movement is not as strong as it should be. But he said it's moving, and it's a yeasty feeling that's coming.

Maybe we should remember the growth of the labor movement, of the civil rights movement, of the women's movement, and recognize that we may be witnessing the growth of a new movement designed to meet the human and consumer needs in our growing technological, computerized society. My advice is for us to not fight it but to get with it.

JENNINGS RANDOLPH: We come together in a time of reflection, but our interest should be in the future, because all of us will spend our lives there, no matter how days would pass or years would come.

I have served for and with nine Presidents of the United States.

The lasting legacy of Franklin Roosevelt and the New Deal is that he and his administrations changed American thinking on the role of government.

In his first inaugural address, FDR declared his constitutional duty to recommend the measures that a stricken nation in a stricken world may require. With that declaration and the actions that followed, FDR certainly abolished the idea that government must stand helpless before the iron laws of marketplace economics. The President declared that government could and should act, and FDR acted.

The actions of the New Deal that followed were guided not so much by economic theory as by that consistent moral purpose. That purpose was made explicit when President Roosevelt in his second inaugural address said, "The test of our progress is not whether we add more to the abundance of those who have much. It is whether we provide enough for those who have too little."

The New Deal brought into wide currency the terms of economic and social justice. Very calmly I say these words are not in vogue in some places today. But the concepts that undergirded the New Deal and much of the Great Society legislation—these remain.

They've even been discovered by those officials who came to our U.S. Capital two years ago with the intention of rolling back the government to a pre-New Deal era. They're having difficulty with the issue of fairness, which is what those of us in this gathering call economic and social justice.

The essential legacy of the New Deal for the future is to continue the effort to improve capitalism, to serve the broader interests of society and individual needs. We must bring about, on a basis that will last, the dignity and sustenance of the individual citizen in our democracy.

PANEL DISCUSSION

DOUGLASS CATER, CHAIR: Now the fun begins. And as Bill Rusher has said, this is not a perfectly balanced panel and, therefore, if I show a slight favoritism in the immediate responses to those who are in the minority on this panel, I hope you will be understanding.

I would like to invite President Ford to respond to three ideas that have, it seems to me, been woven through the discussions of these two days.

First is the role of government as "my brother's keeper," or "substituting for me, as an individual, as my brother's keeper"; second, the government's role as banker for the people, investing in talents and, indeed, sometimes in enterprise in order to serve a banking function; and third, government's central responsibility for the economic growth of the nation in terms of playing an active rather than a passive role.

Are we all pragmatists as we approach these questions, or are there basic philosophical differences that divide us as we take the New Deal legacy and look to the future?

GERALD FORD: Well, Doug, before I respond to your specific questions, let me to a degree reiterate what I was saying earlier.

When you're discussing a legacy, I don't believe you should put the person and his policies in the context of the present-day environment. We on this panel sit on a rather easy pedestal to analyze the times, to analyze the role of an individual. In this instance, it's Franklin Delano Roosevelt.

It's my impression that our role gives us a wonderful luxury to reflect on, to praise, or to criticize what was done fifty years ago without necessarily recommending the same kind of legislation for the decade of the 1980s.

If I can repeat something that I mentioned earlier, I'm sure that back in the 1930s there were many, many responsible business people and others who did not want and fought vigorously against the enactment of the Wagner Act. But I'm sure most people today would agree that labor-management legislation was essential at that time, and the only vehicle that was enacted was, of course, the Wagner Act.

Remember, though, that in 1947 or '48, on reconsideration and review of the situation, new legislation came forward to meet the current problems and, in effect, did away with many of the things that were in the Wagner Act. I speak now of the Taft-Hartley Act.

And then, in the 1950s, recognizing a need to continue federal intervention and involvement in labor-management legislation, but recognizing that the Wagner Act was out of date and the Taft-Hartley Act was out of date, Congress came forth with the Landrum-Griffin Bill.

The fact that some of us may have praised or voted for the Taft-Hartley Act or for the Landrum-Griffin Act doesn't necessarily mean that we didn't feel that the Wagner Act was a necessary tool in the 1930s. I praise the legacy of that forward-looking action, but I wouldn't, today, vote for the Wagner Act under any circumstances. It is not the kind of legislation we want in the 1980s.

Now, regarding one of the questions you specifically raised, Doug—whether the government should be our brother's keeper—my own question is, at what level and how?

There is no question at all in my mind that our government has a firm obligation to help those who, for physical or mental or other such reasons, cannot help themselves. That's a mandatory obligation of the federal government alone or in conjunction with state and local governments.

My next question is, having set that group aside, how can you best help those who are capable of helping themselves? In my opinion, a government does not have a mandatory obligation to help those who have a capability to help themselves. Maybe it is obliged to help on a temporary basis but not on a permanent basis. What we have to do is create an environment in this country that will enable those who can help themselves to be the beneficiaries of the current circumstances.

I'm not quite sure I understand the question about government's role as banker for the people, Doug, so I'll turn to the third question.

If my memory is accurate, we didn't have a lot of the tools back in the thirties for government intervention in our economic policies. Certainly the President's Council of Economic Advisers didn't exist. And I'm not sure that the Federal Reserve Board had the authority and the power that it has now. And certainly the Federal Deposit Insurance Corporation didn't exist. I don't believe the Home Loan Bank Board existed. A number of other things that are in place today weren't around then. And so we had a much more free-market-oriented society in the twenties and thirties. A lot of tools were not availiable that ought to be available and ought to be used by the government in a responsible way.

DOUGLASS CATER: President Brademas, in responding to the panel, are we pragmatically divided or are we philosophically divided?

JOHN BRADEMAS: Well, I sense a good deal more consensus than one might have thought. I think it's very significant that so many agree that the major contribution of the New Deal is the principle that there is a positive, affirmative role for government in the society.

President Ford made the point that we can quarrel about the level at which government assistance may be provided and the mechanisms by which it may be provided, but he also said that he would not want to deny the government the tools—and he mentioned the Council of Economic Advisers as one—for policymaking.

I think that we do now have across the country a general consensus that the dimensions of what we call the "welfare state" will continue and ought to continue. I think what is significant about Mr. Reagan's Presidency is that for the first time in a generation, we have a President who I'm not sure would sign his name to that kind of a statement. He has been busy trying to dismantle, in some cases, and significantly weaken in others, many of the fundamentals. And that, obviously, is not a position with which I agree.

I want to make one other point about another theme that has been running through the conference today and yesterday, the am-I-my-brother's-keeper theme. It seems to me that we can in our individual lives as citizens be concerned about other human beings and take part in voluntary activities or be generous philanthropically, but that doesn't mean that we can turn our backs on the appropriate role of government and of other institutions in the society to guarantee a modicum of social justice.

And because the question was put yesterday in theological terms, if I may be forgiven for venturing into that dangerous area, it would seem to me you could make the point that there is a difference between love in the Christian sense and justice. They are not the same thing. We in the legislative business, or in the governmental business, are more in the justice business than we're in the love business. We may be motivated by the Christian love ethic, but our job is to go out and write laws that mean fair taxes, parity for farmers, and so on—we use all those words of justice to describe what it is we're about.

The other point I would make—just to needle Mr. Rusher a little because I think he's been enormously gracious and hasn't uncorked as he might well have done—is that I totally agree with his assault on waste, abuse, and inefficiency. Who can quarrel with that? And I would agree that we should attack those evils in the food stamp program and the welfare program and wherever else they occur.

I would like, however, to see more pieces in his journal about waste, fraud, and abuse coming out of the Department of Defense, where they spill more coming around the 14th Street bridge than the whole Department of Health and Human Services spends in a year.

WILLIAM RUSHER: I think President Brademas will find in the conservative world, generally, some very trenchant criticisms of defense expenditures. The Heritage Foundation did one most recently.

JOHN BRADEMAS: May I say I applaud that. I think it's a very constructive contribution.

WILLIAM RUSHER: I really wanted to offer somthing else at this point, though. As we were discussing whether the government is our brother's keeper, I recalled a remark by then-Governor Reagan of California in about 1970, when I called him as a witness in opposition to an advocates program that provided for a guaranteed annual income. Barbara Jordan will remember this because she was there as a witness on the other side.

I have never forgotten this remark of Mr. Reagan's. Like all shorthand remarks, it can be accused of oversimplification. But it has something to say to this general proposition of whether government should be our brother's keeper.

He said, "I always thought that it was the function of the government to promote the general welfare, not provide it."

I think that's the distinction here.

DOUGLASS CATER: Congressman Kemp, do you want to get in at this point?

JACK KEMP: Well, I would from the standpoint that I think it's important to recognize that you cannot measure generosity or compassion in a society totally by how many people need the help of the government. Providing the opportunity for people truly to be their brother's keeper, as a biblical injunction, seems to me a more logical role for government.

In other words, a more noble charity, a more noble love, a more noble Judeo-Christian principle is to prevent people from having to take charity in the first place. It seems to me the government also has a responsibility to allow us, as individual Americans, the opportunity to be our brother's keeper and to move toward being a society in which generosity is not measured just by how many people need help. It's also measured by how many people do not need help.

And in that sense, you could look back at the seventies, Mrs. Keyserling, and come to the conclusion that inflation did more to destroy the food stamp program and Aid to Families with Dependent Children and student loans and opportunities for people to go to college or get a home. It seems to me that a doubling of the Consumer Price Index from 1971 to 1980, with inflation running at 12 or 13 percent, would do more to reduce the level of wages, the level of income, the level of benefits, the opportunity to help people help themselves. In fact, Keynes himself said, "There is no surer nor more direct way of overthrowing the basis of an existing free society than for a government to debase the currency."

Now, lest it be said that I am only concerned about fighting inflation, or protecting people from the debasement of the currency, let me add that it seems to me that government also has to create a climate in which you can fully employ the resources, both tangible and spiritual, that we were talking about. Removing those impediments, changing tax laws, and providing for a less-regulated market economy are not, by definition, acting in the disinterest of people.

As impersonal as it might sound, sometimes the market protects the consumer, Ms. Peterson, a lot better than the government can. Which did more for the consumer—regulating the price of energy to a point at which we were standing in gas lines for two-and-a-half hours, or reducing the regulatory burden and encouraging the production of energy?

Just one last point. Mrs. Keyserling reminds us that people produce because people buy. I think that is a contribution of the Keynesian legacy of the New Deal, and I would buy that. As a "supply-sider," I recognize that people produce because people buy. But I also recognize that people produce for the reward that they get for their labor. If you take away the reward for labor, if you take away the reward for investment, if you take away the reward for saving and producing, then ultimately, no matter how much purchasing power is out there, you are going to get less of that which has been promoted.

I will conclude with this supply-side statement by Franklin Roosevelt, from his fireside chat on economic conditions in 1933: "As national income rises, let us never forget that government expenditures will go down and government tax receipts will go up." There is no more important goal of policymaking today in our country, as President Ford said, than to provide for an increase in the national income so that we can remove those government expenditures that are needless as people go to work and can provide for themselves. And the tax revenues will go up as this nation goes back to work.

I think that approach is going to be successful. I certainly hope it is. If it isn't, the very tide that swept people in in '80 will sweep them out and you won't have to worry about it, Mrs. Keyserling.

But if it does work—this pragmatic experiment of trying to expand the national income of this country and keep inflation down while raising employment and output and production—then I would suggest that the same democratic forces at work in 1932 that changed this country might very well be a ratification of that experiment. I think the jury is still out.

JENNINGS RANDOLPH: Mr. Rusher, you said something

about the Sahara Desert, and I just want to ask you if you think that we of the New Deal in 1935 did something wrong when we created the soil conservation service in this country.

WILLIAM RUSHER: Well, I'm trying to relate that to my remark about the Sahara Desert, Senator, without getting into a detailed analysis of soil conservation that I am not prepared for.

The basic point was that government has been found, by experience, by actual observation, not to be in certain large respects all that competent. And I know why, because I, too, run a business, a little magazine in this case, and since it has an annual deficit like the federal government and makes it up by getting money from others—again like the federal government—it is in its way a microcosm.

Over twenty-five years in that business, I've discovered that there's a thing I call "negative economics." Both my *National Review* and the government of the United States run on it, and I'll tell you how it works.

If you have a business that is making a big profit, and one of your employees comes to you and says, "I want to buy a Xerox machine. We can do thus, thus, and so, if we get a new one," you say, "Okay." You've got the money for that.

If you are absolutely on the ragged edge of breaking even and somebody asks you that, you say, "No," because you can't afford it.

But if you're going to lose a heck of a lot of money anyway, the answer is, "Why not?"

And that's what I was getting at.

JENNINGS RANDOLPH: Mr. Cater, you were very kind to refer to the constitutional amendment for eighteen-, nineteen-, and twenty-year-olds to vote. I offered that first in 1942. Only one state—Georgia—had that younger voting age at that time.

I think it's very important for us today to realize the shocking voting situation in our country. Not only is this youth group not voting in our election process, the American people are not voting. In the last general election, in 1980, it was the minority of the majority that voted in this country, that actually elected a President of the United States.

Take the Empire State of New York, where only forty-eight out of every one hundred eligible voted. Across this country, the picture is the same—22 percent of those aged eighteen, nineteen, and twenty voted in that election.

Then I talked to the Ambassador from New Zealand. It made me almost cringe, because he said in New Zealand, where the voting booth is not just around the corner, "we vote 92 percent and there are no penalities attached."

I say to you that somehow or other we have to do something about the failure of the American people to vote on election day. John Kennedy said it was appalling, the lack of the use of the vote by the American people. I just hope that every individual in this room, regardless of his feeling about this or that subject, will leave this program saying, "My vote, if it is not used, ceases to exist."

MARY KEYSERLING: I want to reply to Congressman Kemp's reference to Roosevelt's comment that we need to reduce government expenditures. We do, but we have a few expenditures to make before we can reduce them.

Go back to '33, '34. We spent five or six billion those two years for works projects. Prices are five times higher now. That means we spent twenty-five or thirty billion dollars for work creation and job creation. And relative to GNP today, it was a terribly small sum.

And so I hope when you Congressmen and Senators go back to Congress you will find that $4.6 billion expenditure for job creation far too small. If you want to reduce unemployment, I think you have to think in terms of twenty-five or thirty billion or even forty, and then we can reduce government expenditures drastically, and I think we can reduce inflation drastically.

JACK KEMP: Mrs. Keyserling, with all due respect to your very important comment on the jobs bill, it seems to me axiomatic in a society to recognize that there are other elements of creating jobs. Indeed, the statement could be made that you cannot create employees without first creating employers, that the ultimate source of jobs in our economy does not come from the government. Only one out of every five Americans is now working on the public payroll.

It seems to me that it is important, at this point in our history, if the New Deal legacy is to work and survive and if the Great Society is to work, to have a private sector capable enough, profitable enough, to afford that type of expenditure. The government is expending, in 1984, well over seven-hundred billion dollars. We also have to recognize that there must be an economy productive enough, with a savings pool and a capital pool and a work pool, to afford it.

It also seems important to me to recognize that that jobs bill, as important as it is, is a drop in the bucket. If unemployment were to drop from 10.5 percent to 6 percent, where it should be, or to 5 percent or to full employment, which I believe we have to have in this country, it would not have been the result of government-sponsored jobs. If the government were to do it, as opposed to the private sector, it seems to me that it would totally erode the national income of this country.

I stood up with William Jennings Randolph when President Reagan said that government must create the climate, or government must take action. I think it is absolutely critical that government take action. But I also think that government has to take the right action, and any action at all is not necessarily productive. Sometimes it's counterproductive.

VERNON JORDAN: I want to associate myself with what President Ford just said about times then and times now.

Somebody wrote that new occasions teach new duties; time makes ancient good uncouth. I think that is applicable. I think it is also applicable that government by its very nature is not an initiating body. Government by its very nature is a responding body. The New Deal may be to some extent an exception, but it was responding to a real economic crisis in the country.

What I find very interesting, as I sit here and listen, is, number one, that my friend Jack Kemp would admit at this time that he is still a supply-sider, supply-side economics having supplied more misery, more unemployment, and more deficit. But Jack is an honest man, and I'm glad that he is still admitting to it, despite all of the difficulty it has caused us.

I also found it interesting that my friend Mr. Rusher, whom we've met on other occasions, chose to single out food stamps and talk about food stamp abuse. And then Jack said something that was extraordinary. He said that it was inflation that cut the food stamp program, and I don't think that's right.

But what I want to say to you about the food stamp program and the food stamp people and all of that is you all ought to pick on somebody your size and leave them alone. I mean that. Leave them alone. They're hungry, weak.

On the notion between promoting the general welfare and providing the general welfare, you can debate it all you want to. To the extent that the general welfare has been dealt with historically in this country, it has been dealt with inequitably and based on arbitrary factors, and we ought to recognize that and understand that.

FROM THE AUDIENCE: As I view the shifting industrial base of our country going back to the primary factors of production and moving into the highly competitive technological field, I was wondering if one of the members of the panel would like to posit a modern New Deal program that would deal with our current severe unemployment problem.

JOHN BRADEMAS: In my judgment, we will need to invest far more—not necessarily through direct expenditures, although that will be part of it, but through tax incentives—to encourage more attention to education at every level.

Also, I think that if one looks at the difficult competitive position of the United States in the world economy, there can be no doubt that one of the reasons is that we are not manufacturing products of high enough quality.

I was struck by Mr. Rusher's observations on the incompetence of government. I'm sure that given the size of government, one can find many such instances. But I come from the Midwest, and I don't think I would ascribe extraordinary managerial competence to the automotive industry or to the steel industry in my state.

I think also that we have to target our tax policies much more effectively than was represented in the big Tax Cut Act of 1981. We should target them toward stimulating investment in those sectors of our economy where we can anticipate the highest payoff instead of providing general across-the-board tax cuts that lead to a great deal of financial speculation rather than increased investment in the productive sector.

The other point I would make is this: I find it extraordinary that we can contemplate spending 1.6 trillion dollars on the defense budget in the next five years—and in my years in Congress I never voted against a defense appropriations bill—while at the same time substantially reducing monies that make it possible for us to educate the scientists, the technicians, the managers, the engineers we have to have in order to implement that budget. That seems to me to be lunatic.

So I just come back to my original point, that at least one response to the future of the American economy will be a substantially increased investment in education, science, research, development, technology.

GERALD FORD: John, let me just throw in a comment. I happen to support the 1.6-trillion-dollar defense program. My difference with President Reagan is not in the amount or in the weapon systems. I happen to believe it would be smarter and better to extend that program over six years rather than five years. I don't know what's so sacrosanct about achieving that result in five years.

I feel very strongly that we have to do certain things defense-wise. And as you know, I was a hawk, I am a hawk, and I expect to be a hawk, and I have no apology for it. Now, having said that, I think it's fair to point out that even with the 1.6-trillion-dollar expenditure proposed over the five-year period, that amount will never exceed 29 percent of our total annual federal expenditures.

Let's turn the coin around. All of these programs that are aimed at helping us domestically—entitlement programs, transfer programs, whatever you want to call them—represent about 42 percent of our total annual federal expenditures. So while the Defense Department is gradually getting larger as a percentage of the total pie, our domestic programs are still maintaining a ratio of over 40 percent of our total annual expenditures.

In the main there have been increases in the some three hundred programs in the federal government aside from the Defense Department. The difference is there has been a reduction in the rate of growth.

In other words, instead of those programs growing at 17, 18, or 19 percent per annum, the rate of growth has been cut down to something in the range of 5, 6, or 7 percent. The expenditures have been larger, but they haven't grown as rapidly as all of the previous proponents wanted them to grow. Now, on a selective basis, some can grow more and some can grow less. But our domestic programs are still the biggest chunk out of our annual expenditures for the federal government.

V

CONCLUSION

ELSPETH ROSTOW
CHARLES S. ROBB

CONFERENCE SUMMARY

ELSPETH ROSTOW: I would like to make one comment about what we have heard: the tides of American politics move slowly.

For a very long time, from the foundation of the Republican Party in the 1850s and its first victory in 1860, the standing strength of the Republican Party dominated our politics. Not in every election, but more Americans thought of themselves as Republicans than as Democrats. This was true, with a slight exception, from 1860 to 1932.

We now look at the next great tide of American politics, the period of the so-called Roosevelt Coalition, which started with the election of '32, was emphasized by the election of '36, and has left the majority of Americans identifying themselves with the goals of the Democratic Party, and more specifically, with the set of programmatics which we associate with the name "New Deal."

Each President who has run as a Republican for the last twenty years has either in public or in private hoped that realignment could occur and that we would go back to the better days when the majority of Americans voted right, voted GOP, voted Republican. This hope was articulated very clearly by Mr. Nixon in '72, who asked for realignment around the principles of Republicanism with which he was identified. Indeed, many scholars in 1980 felt that realignment had occurred, and some believe we still don't know but that it may have done so.

What we have assessed, then, is a fifty-year period when the ideas of this tidal Democratic wave have been first established, and then developed, modified, and certainly attacked. We have heard, however, not just one New Deal discussed. Here are the "New Deals" which we have heard in this conference.

First, the participants' New Deal. This could from time to time have sentimental overtones, evocative overtones, and extremely moving overtones. We have received—particularly in the words of James Roosevelt—a sense of what the New Deal looked like through the White House itself. But beyond that, we have heard others who helped formulate New Deal policies and who had the participant sense of the need for these changes and their importance.

Then we had a variety of academic perspectives on the New

Deal. The historians' view ranged across the ideological spectrum and emphasized different aspects of the New Deal. The economists' New Deal emerged as a set of programs relating to an economy manifestly in need of assistance in the period when Franklin Roosevelt was first elected. The lawyers viewed the New Deal as a constitutional period when changes were made—some long overdue, but not all of them. There were protests among participants that the New Deal did not go far enough in some directions—protecting minorities, for example.

And that brings me to the next New Deal. We had a minority's view of the New Deal, portrayed as a period when the rights of specific sects within this country were heeded and when programs were directed toward their cries.

The minority approach was not unlike the approach of a woman's New Deal, a period when women began to become an active part of the body politic as they had not been, even after the amendment in 1920, which had given them the vote.

We also heard about the artists' New Deal, the New Deal as a time when extraordinary things could happen and when drama critics could meet their reward.

But more than that, it was shown to be a time when programs were directed to those in need, whether white, brown, or black; whether male or female; whether artists or laborers; whether on the farm or in the cities.

All these views were matched by those who were critics, who provided a critic's New Deal. To the critic, who described the entire effort as inappropriate, undesirable, and deplorable, the New Deal looks oddly dissimilar to the very "New Deals" which I have just been itemizing.

There were others. But we have seen that the New Deal is a protean concept and that it may be viewed through a set of prisms.

Where did we agree?

We agreed that something of great importance happened— whether desirable or undesirable, whether it went as far as it should, or whether there were still things left undone. We have heard that there are elements of continuity that link the New Deal with subsequent eras. Specifically, these legacies are the programs— the tools, as President Ford so aptly described them—to deal with social, economic, and public problems. Many new tools were

146   V. CONCLUSION

created and not all were appreciated, but they continue to exist in one form or another to this day. The changes undergone by these elements of continuity—the changes particularly in what President Brademas referred to as the "wicked rebellion of 1980"—are yet to be thoroughly assessed and are incompletely understood for the simple reason that we understand the past a bit better, even if we differ, than we understand the meaning of the present.

After having examined the meaning of this fifty years of history, we need to turn to someone who will talk to us about the meaning of the New Deal, to a working politician, to someone in the same party as Franklin Roosevelt, but with a new career.

Charles Robb was born after the New Deal had ended, when Mr. Win-the-War had just about taken over. He was born, then, into a world where most of what we have discussed was already on the books. But he also has lived effectively in a world where the New Deal has been a present reality.

Chuck Robb was educated at the University of Wisconsin, and he served in the Marine Corps from his graduation from that university in 1961 until 1970. He resumed his education and received a law degree from the University of Virginia in '73, and was in practice from then on until his election as Lieutenant Governor of Virginia in '78. He was elected Governor of that state in 1980.

It is then to the Governor of the State of Virginia that I turn this microphone over, and I do so with the greatest pleasure.

PRESERVING THE LEGACIES OF THE NEW DEAL

CHARLES S. ROBB

I believe that the crowded events that have filled the half-century in the life of modern America that we celebrate today represent an important challenge, linking those of us whose profession is politics with those of you whose profession is history. In our common efforts to understand the past, your influence upon the members of my profession may be even greater than you imagine.

Most politicians read history, and all politicians certainly should, because the historian and the politician have at least one thing in common. The historian who understands the relationship between cause and effect has the opportunity to write about history, while the politician who fathoms that connection has the chance to make history.

In addition, the politician who really thinks seriously about the proposition has to consider history invaluable, since the lessons it provides in abundance may be applied with beneficial results to the conduct of public affairs at every level.

Moreover, in the secrecy of our egos, those of us who look over our shoulders to the past also look forward to the future in the hope of favorable disposition at the hands of authors of the biographies and monographs to come, or at least to the semi-obscurity of burial in the explanatory footnotes that adorn those works.

As we look back into the past, and as we try to see ahead into the future, it seems to me that those of us in public life can proceed with a perspective larger and more useful to the tasks of government if we take time to reflect upon what the New Deal means in the larger context of American history in relation to the specific issues and problems we face today. Though I do not pretend to possess the range of knowledge of the historian or the specialized familiarity of the student of the New Deal, I do believe that among all the great domestic developments in America in this century, none has had a more pervasive effect upon the life of the nation than the New Deal. The New Deal was an original and extraordinary reaction to an unprecedented social, economic, and psychological crisis.

The first hundred days of FDR's first term were a bold experiment in government action, unsurpassed before or since in the break that they represented with the past and in the enduring influence they had upon the decades that followed. Unburdened by the enshackling dogmas of an era ending, as his predecessor had been, Franklin Roosevelt set in motion sweeping initiatives that immediately saved the Republic from almost certain economic collapse and the incalculable consequences of social and political upheaval that would have come with it.

At the same time, I think one can argue that the New Deal also provided the solid basis for almost five decades of economic and industrial expansion, for a national resolve sufficient to master a global conflict of unparalleled danger, and for a rebirth of confidence in the principles of government that are necessary to sustain American commitments as a world power in a postwar age of international tension and uncertainty.

The fabric of the New Deal, like other first-rate durable material that can be altered to fit the changes that time works upon the physique, still covers the body of the Republic, from the emergency legislation of the first hundred days that saved the nation's homes and farms; to the first important initiatives in what became in that long and as-yet-unfinished struggle for civil rights; to the federal government's enormous achievements in regional development, agricultural stabilization, conservation, transportation, unemployment compensation, and industrial regulation; to what is probably the greatest achievement of all, Social Security, which Frances Perkins, with some understatement, declared to be "a fundamental part of another great step forward in that liberation of humanity which began with the Renaissance."

The list of permanent legacies left by the New Deal is, of course, much longer, and it is more accurately reflected in the papers that were presented here during the last two days. Yet, from the perspective of one who now serves as a governor, I see in a number of current national issues problems that I am convinced we will have to address if we are to preserve the more important of the legacies passed on to us by the New Deal.

The New Deal altered and expanded the activities and the obligations of the federal government that affect American life, and revised and enlarged the American people's expectations of their national government. For more than forty years the flow of power and the stream of anticipation has been from throughout the land to Washington, and the responsibilities for supporting the programs and obligations that have expanded constantly since the New Deal have flowed back from Washington through the state houses to communities and people throughout the land.

But those directions are now changing. The relationships between the federal and state governments are changing. The federal government's historical financial commitments are being modified or reduced, and in some cases, eliminated altogether.

Now, whether or not we agree with all of the criticisms leveled by what some, in my judgment, simplistically brand "big government," it is my personal feeling that we must maintain the historic commitments that were begun fifty years ago to an active, inclusive government, sensitive to its greatest mandate in serving all of the American people. The central issue facing us now, I believe, is that of deciding how we make the changes that must be undertaken and make them in a fashion that will preserve the integrity of the vital programs begun in the New Deal—programs that recent history and public expectation have implanted as permanent features of the American landscape, specifically Social Security and the related programs of public welfare and asssistance that meet vital human needs. The magnitude of that task as it will affect our long-range future is awesome.

Earlier this week, at the National Governors Association meeting in Washington, I listened to former Commerce Secretary Pete Peterson, speaking on behalf of a distinguished bipartisan group of former Treasury and Commerce secretaries who were studying the impact of huge federal deficits on our future, describe the scope of the problem that lies before us in a powerful, convincing presentation.

Pete Peterson outlined a future of federal indebtedness, not in the deficits of hundreds of billions of dollars projected for the years ahead, but in the range of seven trillion dollars of unfunded liabilities now obligating the federal government if it is to continue all of its current programs and activities.

For the immediate future, there is no question in my mind, or for that matter in the mind of any other governor that I know of, that the states are going to have to play a much greater role than they have over the past decades in the support and delivery of services and programs essential to the people in communities everywhere. And the states can, by virtue of the resources and facilities that they have now, undertake greater responsibilites in the areas of public education, transportation, community economic development, and public safety.

On the other hand, I am convinced, as are the rest of the nation's governors, that the states cannot and should not be called upon to assume burdens that constitutionally and historically the federal government has carried, beginning with the New Deal and the entitlement and income-security programs.

As these programs have expanded in recent decades in the services of Medicare and Medicaid, in Aid for Dependent Children, in the assistance offered the needy through food stamps, they have been developed at the federal level to address pressing needs that are national in scope, needs conditioned by the changing national economic circumstances that only the federal government has the power and the resources to address, conditions that only the federal government, through its economic and financial policies, can influence and ameliorate.

Clearly, this seems to me to have been one of the major conclusions drawn by the authors of the New Deal as they looked at the forces that condition and change the nation's economic life and tried to decide how the federal government could work to keep these forces harnessed to the nation's best interests. The use of federal deficit spending developed during the New Deal was, it seems to me, a technical financial device intended to stimulate growth and expansion in real social investments, in human and community developments that generated real and predictable returns to American society, both economically and psychologically.

While the tactic worked well then, many of us now in public service at the state level—and I am very definitely included in that number—simply don't believe that we can afford to continue with the huge federal deficits that we have now, and certainly that we are facing in the future, and still have any hope of serving either the needs of the American people or the long-range economic interests of the country. This conclusion is confirmed, in my judgment, by the statistics Pete Peterson and his group have marshaled in support of their view of the problems that we now face.

I believe that we have no real choice. The federal deficits simply have to be brought down, and bringing them down will be painful. The problem has reached such proportions that the National Governors Association earlier this week called upon the Administration and upon Congress to reduce spending in the so-called uncontrollable or untouchable categories in the federal budget—defense spending and the non-means-tested entitlement programs specifically.

Until now, these politically sensitive areas of the budget, which comprise approximately 80 percent of the annual spending of the federal government, have been immune from the cutting that the Administration has undertaken in the remaining 20 percent of the federal budget, specifically in the so-called controllable expenditures that include the federal-state programs and the assistance that the federal government provides directly for state and local governments.

Perhaps the dimensions of the current problem are most graphically illustrated by a hypothetical example that some of you have probably heard before. If the federal government chose to pay only its obligations to defend the nation, support the current entitlement programs, and honor the interest payments on the national debt, and eliminated all of the rest of the federal budget and shut down the national government, cold, there would still be a federal deficit. That is how far federal expenditures have gotten ahead of federal revenues.

In my judgment, if we hope to preserve the social and economic gains America has made over the past forty years and keep the great commitments made by at least five Administrations during those decades, we're going to have to take action—tough, painful action—to bring our spending in balance with our means. In short, unless we direct the national dialogue to the question of giving up something, we may run the risk of losing everything.

Beyond these concerns, however, there are deeper, even more

basic questions about our current direction in national affairs that give me pause. They're philosophical in nature.

Beginning with FDR's first Administration, our national government came to look upon the American people as important assets, not as expensive liabilities. The prevailing philosophy of the New Deal was developed in the spirit that it was only natural for the most powerful nation ever on earth to apply its might and the abundance of its resources to assist those of its citizens genuinely unable to help themselves.

Animating that spirit in the unprecedented energies of this New Deal era was the powerful conviction that a representative government, chosen by the confidence of a free people, is not inherently or naturally evil, inefficient, or inept, but in the hands of men and women of vision, generosity, and good will, can be an effective partner of society in the generation of good and the advancement of progress. In that sense, the New Deal sought to represent all of the American people by intervening positively and decisively in virtually every area of the American economy, to bring about as rapidly as possible a real recovery from the shambles of the Great Depression.

As a result, the New Deal, as anyone now in public life should realize, was not aimed solely at helping the helpless, feeding the hungry, sheltering the homeless, and providing jobs for the unemployed. The New Deal, it seems to me, ultimately was critical to the preservation of the stable social and economic center of American life. In that respect the New Deal defied temporary ideological labels. Those who developed it, like FDR, looked upon government as an ally, a willing partner and protective supporter of American society and institutions, the forerunner, if you will, of the public-private partnership that is the goal of so many of us in public life today.

Moreover, contemporary critics of big government failed to perceive that the New Dealers did not presume that the federal government could or should undertake to solve all the problems of all the people always and everywhere throughout this country. Instead, as I believe history has clearly demonstrated, the New Deal sought to target those problems that the complexities of modern industrial society had simply placed beyond the abilities of individual Americans to control. They presumed that the federal government could and should make an effort to solve those problems by changing or controlling the conditions that would cause the recurrence of economic ruin.

From my perspective the New Deal was an experiment, inspired by the powerful tradition of experiment in American life. As the master experimenter responsible for the New Deal, Franklin Roosevelt was superbly equipped for the unique rigors that came with that task. He succeeded because he was bold, sensing instinctively and overwhelmingly that the unprecedented economic crisis gripping the nation demanded action, whatever the risks and no matter the dangers. He also succeeded, I believe, because his courage, both as a politician and as a leader, was complemented by the kind of vision that both stimulated and was stimulated by experimentation.

Finally, it is my own feeling that the experiment of the New Deal worked because America is essentially an experiment, an experiment in the continuing search for equipoise between those things in American life which are organic and ever changing and those things in our nation's experience which are immutable and unchanging. To strike that delicate balance is to produce the resonance of continuing American progress. FDR struck that balance because he had the greatness of spirit, the capaciousness of intellect, and the boundless confidence in the future of America that made him unafraid to ask the right questions to find the right answers, to risk being grossly wrong in the venture of being grandly right.

And he had something else, something ultimately even more important. He had the unshakeable convictions—transparently obvious in both word and gesture—that so easily and naturally charged with electric vibrance all of his communications with the American people.

Like the man to whom this library is dedicated, Franklin Roosevelt was a people's President. That in the end may have weighed more in the balance of the success of the New Deal than any other single element. If it did, then for those of us now serving in government, the example and the inspiration of why it did is not hard to find.

Finally, among all of the memorable things he said, the lines in Franklin Roosevelt's career that I find most helpful, lines of timeless beauty and transcendent wisdom, are the lines he uttered in accepting the Democratic nomination for reelection in 1936. With these lines I close:

> Governments can err; Presidents do make mistakes. But the immortal Dante tells us that divine justice weighs the sins of the cold-blooded and the sins of the warm-hearted on different scales. Better the occasional faults of a government that lives in a spirit of charity than the constant omissions of a government frozen in the ice of its own indifference.